Christi Youd

Organize Your Office for Success

A busy person's guide to keeping your office organized with minimum maintenance

www.OrganizeEnterprise.com

ORGANIZE
Enterprise™

Table of Contents

Introduction i

Chapter 1:   Boosting Your Productivity   1

FIRST STAGE – Control your workflow using one, singular
system 5
SECOND STAGE – Create an environment that improves
your concentration 5
THIRD STAGE – Clarify your targets and move straight
toward them 6

Chapter 2:   Processing Your Workflow   11

One singular system- tickler file / follow up form 11
Gather it into your processing system 13
Filter it through your five options 14

**Work Less, Produce More: 5 Steps to Delegating with
Authority   15**
Prioritize daily 21

Your First Priority -- Prioritize!   22
Act on your priorities.. 25
Mastery of skills 26
Make your system portable 27

Chapter 3:   E.N.D. C.H.A.O.S.   31

Clutter in your environment 32
Clutter in your mind 32
Clutter in your schedule... 33

Chapter 4:   Why Do You Want to Get Organized?   37

Chapter 5:   What is Happening?   39

Chapter 6:   What Do You Want to Have Happen?   47

Chapter 7:   What is Causing the Disorganization?   57

Chapter 8:   Design Your Plan   65
Design with your target(s) in mind 65
Create cockpits for workstations.. 66
Coordinate activities, supplies, and containers 71
Respond to your examination... 71

Chapter 9:   Categorize Your Things & Haul Them to Their Destination   75
Categorizing Paperwork 75

Chapter 10:   Assign the Right Home for Everything   81
Assigning Homes for Paperwork 81
Assigning homes for electronic files 84
Assigning homes for things that belong in a drawer........... 84
Assigning Homes for Things that Don't Belong in a Drawer87

Chapter 11:   Obtain the Right Container for Everything 89
The Right Container for Paperwork 90

Option A: Smead Viewable Labels   91

Option B: Avery Labels   92
Labeling 96

Chapter 12:   Sustain Your System   97
Daily Maintenance 97

Chapter 13:   Goal Setting   101
Consider your target(s)... 102
Align your activity to hit the target..................................... 106

Chapter 14:   Knowing How to Do It   109

Chapter 15:   See Your Targets Clearly in Both Your Conscious and Subconscious Mind   115

Chapter 16:   Organizing Your Neuro-Associations: Financial Pain   121

Chapter 17:   Organizing Your Neuro-Associations: Mental Pain   127

Chapter 18:   Organizing Your Neuro-Associations:
Social Pain   131

Chapter 19:   Organizing Your Neuro-Associations:
Emotional Pain   135

Chapter 20:   Organizing Your Neuro-Associations:
Spiritual Pain   137

Chapter 21:   Organizing Your Neuro-Associations:
Physical Pain   141

Chapter 22:   Organizing Your Neuro-Associations: Mixed
Associations   145
   The Freedom of a Structured Schedule   146

Chapter 23:   Organizing Your Neuro-Associations:
Financial Pleasure   155

Chapter 24:   Organizing Your Neuro-Associations:
Mental Pleasure   159

Chapter 25:   Organizing Your Neuro-Associations:
Social Pleasure   163

Chapter 26:   Organizing Your Neuro-Associations:
Emotional Pleasure   167

Chapter 27:   Organizing Your Neuro-Associations:
Spiritual Pleasure   169

Chapter 28:   Organizing Your Neuro-Associations:
Physical Pleasure   171

Chapter 29:   Organizing Your Neuro-Associations: Mixed
Associations   175

Chapter 30:   Your Conscious and Subconscious Mind 179
   Your subconscious mind 181

Chapter 31:   Organizing Your Mind   183
   Tangible pictures 209

Chapter 32:   What You Accomplish by Mental Conditioning   **212**

    Daily Conditioning.. 213
    Share your vision 213
    Stay true to your course 214
    The Typical Organized Workday 214
    Working with Your Processing System............................. 215
    Compressing Your Activity 215
    The End of Each Day 216

About the Author 217

Introduction

As a professional organizer and productivity consultant, I have spent years helping people get themselves and their offices organized and boost their productivity. I have recognized a need to provide assistance to people whose abilities lie somewhere in between doing it themselves and hiring a professional consultant to come in and do it with them. I saw the need for a set of written instructions on how to boost productivity at work, instructions that can help people thrive in the workplace, increasing their productivity to the point they are able to achieve their greatest career goals and aspirations.

The names in my case studies have been changed in order to protect the innocent or the guilty as the case may be. The case studies included in this book are a representation of a large collection of clients, students, acquaintances, and ideas.

I married a man whose surname was Youd. My maiden name was Miller. All my life I planned on naming my children unique and original names. My husband grew up determined that all his children's names would be easy to read and properly pronounce. (It's amazing how many ways people pronounce Youd). We spent the entire nine months of each pregnancy debating the child's name. When I was in the final trimester of our first child's pregnancy I was a fan of a soap opera that the main character was a man by the name of Drake. I liked it so one morning I presented the idea to my husband. We sat across from each other at the breakfast table. He was in a suit and tie and I was still in my pajamas. I said I liked the name Drake for our child. My husbands face scrunched up and he looked at me as though that was the stupidest thing he had ever heard and proclaimed loudly, "That's a duck!! We are not naming our child a duck!" It's funny what you associate to a name isn't it. He, the mighty hunter, associated it to game. I, the mighty soap opera enthusiast, associated it to a hunk on CBS. We named our child Trevor. It's probably for the best. But now I'm writing a book and I need to use fictitious names to protect the innocent. I find myself at last being able to name someone the unique and creative names I aspired to. Therefore the name I will give the character for our main case study will be Drake. Will that be Drake the duck or Drake the hunk? You'll have to decide.

Organize Your Office for Success

Drake is a man in his mid 30's who is married and has three children. Drake likes to jog, ski, and hike. He watches football on the

weekends. His wife adores him. Drake dotes on his wife. His children excel in school but not in sports. Drake lives in a quiet subdivision where it is safe to leave your door unlocked during the day. He is a partner in a thriving mid-sized company. He has 80+ employees and more business then his company can keep up with. Drake didn't think of himself as disorganized. Sure he had clutter in his office but who didn't. Drake had file drawers full of paper and six or seven piles that were six inches high throughout his office space.

Drake and I were assessing whether or not there was a way I could help him boost his productivity and thus improve his bottom line. I asked Drake to track a few things over a 30 day period. I asked him to track how much time he spent looking through his piles and files looking for the things he needed in order to do his work. He tracked it. He found he averaged eight minutes per hour digging through things looking for what he needed. That meant that in an eight hour work day he was wasting one full hour a day.

We organized Drake's mental processes, office space, and work process system as explained in this book and found it decreased the amount of time he spent looking for things. He tracked it after we implemented the changes and found he only spent one to two minutes per hour looking for the things he needed. This boosted his productivity by 12%.

I asked Drake to monitor his ability to concentrate on his work. He tracked the number of distractions he experienced in a day. Distractions such as email or telephone calls, people stopping by the office, seeing something on his desk that reminded him of something else he needed to do, thoughts cycling through his mind of things he needed to be sure to remember, delays in meetings or meetings going too long, etc. Drake found he averaged over 90 distractions a day. On average each distraction took two minutes to deal with. We consolidated and streamlined the distractions using the methods taught in this book. He found he cut the number of distractions in half and reduced the time needed for each remaining distraction by 75%. That means he used to waste three hours a day dealing with distractions where as now he only spends 22 minutes a day dealing with them. This boosted his productivity by another 30%.

Drake was already successful in business so he was obviously doing some things right. However I sat him down and asked him what the activities were that impacted the bottom line and how much of his time was he dedicating to those activities. He was surprised to realize that he only spent 10% of his efforts on the activities that had the greatest impact on the bottom line. We mapped out a plan of how he could set up his office space to support the activities that were the most important in his business and Drake started spending 40% of his time doing the activities that made the greatest impact to his bottom line. Now Drake not only had more time. He was spending his time on the right activities. This boosted his productivity as well.

Whatever your circumstances I am confident that this book can help you boost your productivity to a higher level. Perhaps 25%! Perhaps 400%! It's all relevant to where you are now and where you want to go.

I have included a number of exercises throughout these instructions. It is important that you, the reader, take time to complete the exercises as you go along. Otherwise, you will miss out on the essential discoveries about yourself and your situation that impact your productivity. Read the book through in its entirety. Complete the exercises as you go along. Apply what you learn throughout the book. If you do this, you will boost your productivity significantly. Enjoy!

Part I

Getting Started

1

Boosting Your Productivity

Imagine your eight hour workday is represented by a two-quart Rubbermaid container. It has a limit to its capacity. It can only hold so many things. You cannot expand your day. It is only so big. Imagine everything that flows into your day, whether they are tasks, phone calls, emails, meetings, paperwork, appointments, or projects are represented by a Lego. There are so many Legos they would overflow a four-quart Rubbermaid container. Your challenge is to get everything that flows into your day – all the Legos in the four-quart Rubbermaid container – to fit within the limits of your eight hour day – the two-quart Rubbermaid container.

Imagine dumping the Legos out of their four-quart container into the two-quart container. Imagine leveling off the top of the container so you can put a lid on it. When I've done this exercise with clients, we have found about 50% of the Legos were left over. In visualizing this analogy, you have represented all activity dumped haphazardly into your day.

Since there is a "lid" on your day, which is the time you need to go home, we need to make these items fit inside the container.

Organize Your Office for Success

Remember, the Legos that were left over represent the things left over that did not get done.

Now, without stretching or distorting the size of the container (since you don't want to increase the number of hours you are spending at work) I want you to use your creativity to do what you can to get as many of these things (Legos) to fit inside your day (two-quart container) as you can. This will represent you getting more done in a day.

The question you have to ask yourself is, "Do you want to keep working where you dump into your day everything you need to do, and then get as much done in whatever haphazard way you can, or do you want to take the time and effort of *organizing all along the way* so you can accomplish more?" It will take some of your time, discipline and effort, so maybe you don't want to bother with it – some people despair at the idea of organizing their time, so they would rather accept the status quo.

Most of the people in my workshops compress the Legos together and stack them neatly in the container side by side in order to fit more of them in. It takes them about 20 minutes. We sit there in silence while they manipulate the Legos. Most people are able to get the other 50% of the Legos into their container.

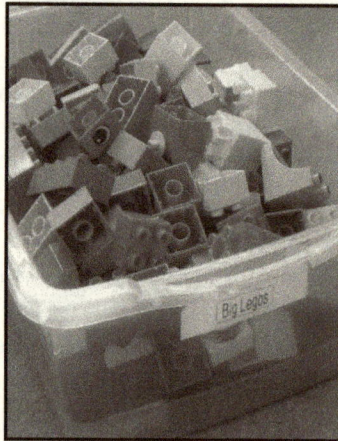

Tasks that flow into your day can be
represented by a Lego.

What lessons can we learn from this?

What can you do to get more things accomplished without increasing the size of your day?

- Seminar participants were able to fit the events into their day by ORGANIZING their activity and by ORGANIZING the flow of things that came to them.

- They had to take some time to do it.

- The organizing had to be done first, and it had to be ongoing.

- Organizing made the impossible become possible (It was impossible to fit all those Legos in before; but by organizing them, it became possible).

- Spending time organizing actually gave them more available time (or space) in their eight hour day.

If your choice is to organize everything along the way so you can get more done in your eight hour day, then you need to recognize that organizing is the only way you are going to fit everything in. If you want to accomplish more, you are going to have to take the time and effort to organize as you go throughout your day. That means filing papers away, putting everything into your tickler system (I'll explain more about that later), keeping your desk clear of everything except the current project you are working on, following a structured schedule, etc. It's the only way to expand your personal work capacity without expanding the number of hours you work in a day. The choice is yours.

Here is my definition of being organized at the office. Each element of the definition contributes to the greater whole. You may find there are some elements that you have already mastered or some elements you have no interest in mastering. However, for our shared quest to help you get truly organized all the elements must be considered and addressed.

- To be organized at the office means you have everything established so you function at your very best, feel great about the way your space and work looks, and so your level of productivity is congruent with your work demands or ambitions.

- To be organized at the office means you have your career goals clearly established in your mind and you have mastered the mental conditioning that drives you to reach those goals.

- To be organized at the office means to have a master plan of what activities will produce the outcomes you desire, have work stations set up to perform those activities, and to have the equipment and supplies that are needed in their appropriate place.

- To be organized at the office means to eliminate the clutter in your office space. It means to eliminate the clutter that runs amuck in your mind. It means to eliminate the clutter that fills your schedule.

- To be organized at the office means you have organized your thoughts, beliefs, what you associate pleasure and pain to, your feelings, and behaviors so they work together to propel you to success.

- To be organized at the office means to have a structured schedule where activities are compressed and organized in a manner that enables you to perform at the height of efficiency and effectiveness. It means you have structured behaviors such as habits and routines that help you be efficient and effective in your work.

- To be organized at the office means to implement systems that minimize your stress and increase your work capacity. It's having systems so well established that you can go on automatic pilot so you can concentrate on your projects not your process. These systems should be set up in such a way that they require the minimum amount of maintenance.

- To be organized at the office means to have a work process flow where work flows into your office, gets processed efficiently and effectively in your office and flows out of your office in a timely manner.

- To be organized at the office means you master management skills. Management of time, task, team, space, information, paperwork, email, interruptions, meetings, delegation, discarding, prioritizing, processing, scheduling, etc. etc. etc.

If your choice is to get organized, you need to do it in three stages:

FIRST STAGE – Control your workflow using one, singular system

Work comes into your office in many formats. Paperwork, emails, voicemail, verbal requests and thoughts from your own mind are the most common formats. Sometimes people fall into the trap of having their office be a storage space for their work to sit until they find time to do it.

It's important that you keep your office space a work *process center* where work:

- enters into your process system as soon as it enters your life or office

- is processed through the system, and

- exits the process when it is completed

As soon as work (in any format) comes into your office, it needs to be processed in one, singular system. People tend to try to manage a different system for every format that comes into their office. They will have one system for paperwork, another system for email, another system for telephone messages, etc. This hurts their level of productivity and causes them to let things slip between the cracks. You want one system that will manage all the formats of incoming work. I'll teach you how.

SECOND STAGE – Create an environment that improves your concentration

The next stage to getting organized so you can boost your productivity is to create an environment that will improve your concentration. You see, if you want to boost your productivity, you must boost your ability to concentrate. If you want to boost your ability to concentrate, you must eliminate distractions. Clutter is a major source of distraction. It can be clutter in your environment, clutter in your mind, or clutter in your schedule.

Have you ever sat down at your desk and seen something sitting there that reminded you of an uncompleted task? Did filing that little reminder away in your mind disrupt your work or thought processes that were already in motion? Sometimes that disruption is just momentary, and sometimes you take a major or minor detour before getting back to the project you were initially working on.

Every paper, pile or thing in your office acts as a distraction and destroys your concentration. As much as possible, it all needs to be well organized and out of sight in order for you to be able to fully concentrate. Later in this book, I will give you step-by-step instructions on how to create a clutter-free and distraction-free environment at work.

THIRD STAGE – Clarify your targets and move straight toward them

What are your business goals and aspirations? If you knew you could not fail, what would you try to achieve? When I do "needs assessments" with clients, I always ask them what their business goals for the next one to five to 20 years are. Occasionally, they will know, but often they will not. When I work with an entire executive team, and I ask the same question to each member of the team individually, it's disturbing how rarely they share common goals. Another word for goals is "targets" and a clearly defined target is easier to hit.

Oftentimes, we go through life like a ping pong ball. We go along our way until something or someone comes into our life and taps us, sending us in a different direction. Then we continue that course until someone or something else comes into our life and taps us, sending us in yet a different direction.

Have you ever been working and received a telephone call that causes you to stop what you were doing and do something else? Have you ever planned your day then had someone else tell you something they needed you to do that day, so you changed your plans? Have you ever started pursuing something and come up against a difficulty that stopped you from pursuing it or caused you to change what you were pursuing? Is your life one endless series of causes that act as ping pong paddles with you acting as the ping pong ball, being bounced from one direction to the next?

If you want to reach your business goals, you have got to take control of your agenda. You have got to keep your mind focused on your desired targets. This can only be done if they are clearly defined. Of course, there are times when a deviation in your course is necessary, but this should be the exception not the rule.

It will take work. It will take effort. You may run into a few challenges along the way. You may have to do some things that are at first foreign to you. You may feel uncomfortable at times as you try to develop new habits. You may even, metaphorically speaking, fall down at some point. Get back up. Keep going. It is so worth it. The benefits of mastering these skills will stay with you for the rest of your life. It will impact not only your life here at work, but your personal life as well. Has there ever been incongruence between what you wanted or needed to accomplish and what you were actually able to accomplish? When you are able to get those two in alignment you'll feel like it was so worth it. Has there ever been incongruence between what time you need to be home at night and what time the work is finished to the point you can leave the office for the day? When you are able to get those two to be compatible you will recognize that all your discipline to get organized is worth it. Have you ever felt stressed at work because of time demands or workload demands? When you go through your days at work with an extremely low level of work related stress you'll be feeling like it's worth it. When opportunities become available to you due to your amazing work capacity it becomes so worth it. When what you are demonstrating at work becomes congruent with who you really are and what you are really capable of, it becomes so worth it.

> **For a free download of our special report "25 Quick Tips to Finally Get Control of Your Messy Environment" visit: www.OrganizeEnterprise.com/25quicktips.**

Part II

First Stage:
Process Your Work

2

Processing Your Workflow

Several years ago, I began a quest. I knew how to organize an office so people could function better, but I had not yet learned how to get a person to *act* in an organized manner. Sure the space stayed organized because of the systems I installed, but the executive working in the space was still wasting a lot of time and money due to their disorganized activity. I spent six months searching for any system, idea, product, or method that would help an executive act in an organized manner. Eventually I found what I believe to be the best system. It's called the GO System. For complete information on using the GO System, or on obtaining GO System products, or on becoming a certified GO System trainer, visit www.thegosystem.com. I can give you the basics of how the system works, but you should purchase their system and reap the full benefit.

One singular system- tickler file / follow up form

This system is a work processing system that uses a tickler file. It transforms your office from a task and paper storage facility into a work processing center–where work comes in, gets processed, and goes out in a timely manner. It makes life a whole lot easier. Just

Organize Your Office for Success

like taking the time to stack your Legos so you can fit more in your container, you have to take time to enter everything into the system, work it through the system, and let work come out of the system in order for you to fit more into your day.

To set up this work processing system, you need to make a tickler file. You need the following:

- a file for each date (31 files numbered 1-31).
- a file for each month (12 files labeled January through December).
- a file for each person in your office that you frequently exchange papers/work with.
- a file for each recurring meeting you have.
- files titled "Follow-up Forms," "Casual Reading," and "Waiting for Response."

Use a follow up form and a tickler file.

Put these files in your most convenient drawer. You are going to be getting into this drawer a lot throughout the day. If you tend to keep everything in an electronic format you will also need a electronic planner that facilitates the tickler system. Use the electronic format for everything except paperwork. Use the physical files for the paperwork.

One of the beauties of this system is that it brings all five streams of incoming work you have been trying to maintain (paperwork, email, voicemail, verbal requests and thoughts from your own mind) and converts them into a singular system. It makes it much easier to stay on top of your workload and much less likely to have things slip between the cracks.

The tool that you use to blend everything into one singular system is a follow-up form. See the sample form below. You can order a supply of these colored, follow-up forms from Organize Enterprise by going to our website at www.OrganizeEnterprise.com. They cost about five cents a sheet, and if you use 20 sheets a day, it will cost you about $1.00 a day to stay highly organized. If you choose to create your own follow-up form, be sure you have visual identity on it. Perhaps have an image on it that makes it stand out. It needs to be very easy to identify as your follow-up form. It represents that an action needs to be taken right away. If has colored ink, it will be easier to identify as well.

Gather it into your processing system

Your work flows to you in five different formats. Paperwork that comes to you representing some task you need to perform is one format. Email is another format. All emails that come to you require action-whether it is an assignment contained in the email, responding to the email, or simply deleting the email. Voicemail is the third format. Voicemail and telephone communications usually represent some sort of task. Verbal requests made to you or verbal information given to you is another format. Finally, thoughts in your own mind remind you of tasks you should do. So, thoughts are the fifth and final format.

That is the gathering phase. You gather your paperwork, email, voicemail, verbal requests and thoughts. Now let me explain the filtering phase.

Filter it through your five options

As each item comes to you, whether it is paperwork, email, voicemail, verbal requests or your own thoughts, you want to filter it through five decisions. The first question you want to ask yourself is, "Can I discard this?" If you are not sure, ask yourself, "Under what circumstances am I going to use it again?" "Can I get it from someone or somewhere else?" Discard as much as you possibly can as soon as you possibly can. Not discarding things quickly enough causes offices to become cluttered and causes *you* to be unproductive.

One tip for mastering the skill of discarding is to first get vividly clear on your one-year, five-year, ten-year, and end-of-career goals. What do you want to accomplish over the next several years? Unless you are vividly clear and very specific on what you are aiming for, you have very little chance of hitting your career targets. Knowing exactly where your career targets are greatly increases the chances of you hitting them. You can align your activity with your desired outcomes.

People tend to fill their day with busy work. It's work that doesn't really further their purpose or their short or long term goals. It is work that meets someone else's agenda not their own. Of course, I'm not talking about work your boss or supervisor assigns you.

If you cannot discard it, filter it through the second decision by asking yourself, "Can I delegate this?" One key to being a highly effective executive is developing effective delegation skills. If it doesn't absolutely have to be performed by you, delegate it to someone else. This is assuming that you are in a leadership position and that you have someone to delegate it too.

When you delegate, write down on a follow-up form exactly what you want the person to do; also write down the exact date and time you want them to report back to you about the matter. Emphasize that reporting back is just as important as getting the task done.

Write on a second follow-up form that you need to follow up with that person the day after you told them to report back to you. You want to give them the full opportunity of shouldering the responsibility of reporting back to you. If they do report back in a timely manner, congratulate them for getting the task done and for reporting back as they should.

You'll put your follow-up form in your tickler system on the appropriate date, which is the date after the date you told them to report back. If you have to seek them out and get the report, make a big deal about it. Reprimand them for not reporting back at the appointed time. Encourage them to do better in the future.

Some other tips for mastering the skill of delegating are to first decide who your best choice is. Give written communication as to who is to complete the assignment, who issued the assignment, what needs to be done, and by what date and time the person responsible for the assignment needs to report back to you. Do this again on a follow-up form.

• If the matter is not pressing, put the written communication into the person's file in your tickler system. Once a day deliver all communication, paperwork, etc. that needs to go to other employees. That way it takes less of your time and you cause fewer interruptions in other people's day.

• If the matter is pressing, simply deliver the written communication and paperwork to the person you are delegating it too.

• If you are the one being delegated to, complete the task in the appointed time, give a written communication to the person who delegated it to you, and deliver the written communication by the appointed time.

Work Less, Produce More: 5 Steps to Delegating with Authority

If you're one of the many business professionals today trying to do more in less time, you know that delegation is a must. Unfortunately, the majority of business people reveal that they dislike delegating. Either they believe the delegated task will "fall through the cracks" and never get done, or that it will get done, but not to their liking. As such, they refuse to delegate anything to anyone unless it's absolutely necessary, and even then they often opt to work longer hours rather than turn the task over to someone else.

Realize, though, that not delegating causes more stress to you and leads others to believe that you don't trust them or don't want them to take on new responsibilities. That's when people view you as a "control freak" who refuses to let anything go.

The good news is that effective delegation follows a simple process that anyone can learn. And whether you're a manager overwhelmed with deadlines and meetings or a business owner trying to stay on time with multiple projects and travel schedules, the following five tips will enable you to delegate effectively and be more productive.

1. Be committed to the full delegation cycle.

Proper delegation is actually a cycle. Think of it like the links of a chain, where each link interacts with others. Every link has four points, just as the delegation cycle does.

- The top of the link intertwines and comes away from the link above it. This represents the task coming to you from some other source, such as a supervisor or customer.
- The link then circles around and interacts with the links next to it and below it. One side of the interaction represents you delegating portions of the assignment to others.
- The other side of the interaction represents you following up to get a report from the people you delegated to.
- Finally, the link completes the cycle and returns to its point of origin. This represents you forwarding the report, decision, or findings to the source that originally gave you the task.

Be sure to complete all four points of interaction with every assignment. If you neglect any of these four points, the link is broken and the chain loses its strength. That's when the delegation process fails.

2. Delegate in writing.

Often the delegation process breaks down because the person being delegated to is unclear on the details of the assignment. And rather than ask you for clarification (and possibly appear incompetent) the person sits on the assignment hoping you'll give some additional clues about what you really want. That's why you need to put every delegated task in writing.

The written document can be a simple e-mail or it can be something more formal, such as a detailed process sheet. The purpose of writing the task out is that it causes you to slow down enough and include all the details someone needs to complete the task successfully. Additionally, your written note provides clarification for the person who receives it. He or she can refer back to your written instructions while doing the task to make sure the work is being done right.

Yes, written delegation takes more time then verbal delegation. However, remember that for every minute you spend writing out the details, you save one hour in execution.

3. Train your team members to report back on time.

In your written instructions, be sure to tell people when you want them to report back to you, both with progress updates and the final product. Be specific. For example, rather than say, "Please give me regular updates on your progress," say, "Please provide me a status update every Friday at 2 p.m. for the next two months, or until the project is completed." And instead of saying, "Finish this by Wednesday," say, "Please complete this task by noon on Wednesday." Being specific removes any guesswork and enables your team to live up to your expectations.

When team members report back on time, make a big deal about it. Thank them for completing the assignment and congratulate them for reporting back within the timeframe outlined. Likewise, when they fail to report back on time, make an even bigger deal about it. Even if they completed the task but didn't report back to you with the final product, help them realize that reporting back is every bit as important as getting the task done. With every delegated assignment, you need to reinforce the importance of reporting back in a timely manner.

4. Use a reminder system to ensure proper follow up.

Never delegate an assignment and completely leave it up to the other person to make sure it gets done. Just as the person you delegate to needs to be accountable for reporting in, you need to be accountable for following up.

Your reminder system can be your daily planner, a tickler file system, or any other system that works for you. Place a note in your reminder system to follow up with a team member if you have not received the report, update, or task as requested. So if you give the team member the deadline of Friday at 2:00 p.m. for a progress update, then you enter into your own reminder system to follow up with the person at 4:00 p.m. if he or she does not meet that deadline. Give the team member the full opportunity to report to you before you track the individual down for follow up.

Important: Only follow up when the person misses a requested update or deadline. You don't want to train people that you will be following up with them on a regular basis, as that leaves the task's responsibility with you. Rather, you want to train them that they are expected to report back to you, making them responsible for the delegated item. That's why you set the progress updates and deadlines in writing. If they don't report as scheduled, you must follow up. If they don't report and you don't follow up, the delegation cycle is broken and the process fails.

5. Report back to the person you received the assignment from.

Just because you receive the delegated task back completed (and to your satisfaction) doesn't mean you're done. Always remember to complete the cycle by reporting back to the person who initially gave you the task. Tell your boss the findings; give the customer the information he or she needed; share your report with the Board. Keep the communication chain in tact so others learn that they can trust you as well.

Delegate to Win

If you want to free up some of your time so you can focus on your core duties or income producing activities, you need to delegate effectively. So examine those tasks that are repetitive in nature and decide which ones someone else can do. Then delegate effectively

Organize Your Office for Success

by writing out your task, training people to report on time, doing proper follow up, and finally completing the cycle and reporting your results. Taking the time to get the delegation process right pays great dividends, in the form of increased productivity, on-track company objectives, and reduced work-related stress.

Visit www.OrganizeEnterprise.com
to subscribe to this newsletter.

If you can neither discard it nor delegate it, filter it through the third decision: "Can I do this in 60 seconds or less?" If you can take care of it in less than 60 seconds, then it's worth your while to stop what you are doing and take immediate action on it.

If it is going to take *longer* than 60 seconds, filter it through decision number four: "Is this something I need to file for follow up?" Meaning you need to take some kind of action with it other than filing it away for future reference. Make the decision as to what date you are going to take that action and file it in the appropriate dated file. If it is to be done in the next thirty days, file it in the numbered file on the date you have selected. If it is something that needs to be acted on during some month in the future, file it in the appropriate file for the month you are going to take action on it.

Let's take each format and illustrate how to enter it into your follow-up files.

You are bringing things from a variety of formats into a singular, consistent format. Now you are no longer trying to manage five systems. You only have to manage one. That way, things do not fall between the cracks or get forgotten.

The follow-up form is the singular, consistent format
you want to create for your process system.

• If the format comes to you as an 8 ½-by-11 sheet of paper or set of papers, attach it to a follow-up form. Write on the follow-up form what you are supposed to do with the paper. Make a decision as to what date you are committed to taking action on this item. File it for follow up in the appropriate dated file.

• If the paper that comes to you is smaller than an 8 ½"-by-11", attach it to a follow-up form. Write on the follow-up form what you are supposed to do with the paper. Make a decision as to what date you are committed to taking action on this item. File it in the appropriate dated file.

• If work comes to you as an email, write down what you need to do for the email on a follow-up form. Make a decision as to what date you are committed to taking action on that email. File it in the appropriate dated file.

• If the format is voicemail, write down what you need to do on a follow-up form. Make a decision as to what date you are committed to taking action on that voicemail. File it in the appropriate dated file.

• If it is a verbal request, write it down on a follow-up form. Make a decision as to what date you are committed to taking action on that verbal request. File it in the appropriate dated file.

• If it is a thought out of your own head, write it down on a follow-up form. Make a decision as to what date you are committed to taking action on that idea. File it in the appropriate dated file.

So making the decision to file it for follow up is the fourth filter in the filtering process. Let's move onto the fifth filter.

• If you determine you don't need to do anything to follow up on the matter, but you want to hold onto it for reference purposes, filter it through the fifth and final decision, which is: "Can I file this in my reference files?" File it away properly in your reference files, *not* in your work processing system files.

We have talked about the gathering process. We have talked about the filtering process. Next, I need to illustrate the prioritizing process.

Prioritize daily

By the time you add all your paperwork, email, voicemail, verbal requests, thoughts, and ideas, your dated files become quite full. Each day at the end of the day, you pull out the following day's file. Lay out every follow-up form on your desk so you can look at all of them at the same time. Determine the most important task you need to accomplish the next day. Turn the follow-up form for that task face down. Decide which task you need to accomplish the next day is the *next* most important. Turn the follow-up form for that task face down on top of the first follow-up form that you turned face down. Continue this process until all the follow-up forms are face down in one neat stack. Put this stack in the file folder so the very most important task is in the front of the file. Hang the file back inside your drawer. You can now go home with your mind free of worry, because you know what you will be doing the next day; and you can rest assured that you will be working on what is truly most important.

Your First Priority -- Prioritize!

Life offers us an abundance of activities and experiences. There is not enough time to do them all. That is why there is such a demand for time management training. One key to managing our time well is to be effective at prioritizing our work. Most executives know the simple strategy of choosing the top priorities to work on the next day and then actively working on those priorities. This is a simple and beneficial strategy. However when we do this randomly we tend to prioritize according to what is most urgent or most intriguing rather than what is most important. Steven R. Covey states that urgent tasks are tasks that need immediate attention. Important tasks are tasks that support you in what you truly value. If you want to boost your productivity and lower your work-related stress you must learn to spend your time on what is most important not on what is most urgent. If you lay some ground work you'll be able to consistently choose the tasks that are the most important. I recommend that you create a master priority list from which to work. Establish a hierarchy of priorities that you can use as a guide.

To establish your hierarchy of priorities you need to first develop your master vision. What do you want your work to stand for? Imagine yourself in the last week of your career. You're cleaning out your office and you stop to reflect on your career. You ask yourself the all important questions, "Did I accomplish what I most needed to accomplish in my work? Did I get to experience what I most wanted to experience?" What would those accomplishments and experiences be for you? It's different for every person. Develop a vision of what you want your work to be about. What you want to accomplish and experience. What your vision is of the ideal career.

Developing your master vision lays initial groundwork of effective prioritizing that allows for a fruitful and productive career. Now you need to build on it. The next layer of effective prioritizing is to establish a hierarchy of priorities for the tasks you need to perform to make your vision a reality.

Edwin created his hierarchy of priorities and divided it into three groups. His top priority group was to provide great customer service to his current customers. He made a list of the activities he typically needed to perform for customers. He prioritized that list so if there was ever more than one customer needing his attention at the same time he knew which task took precedence. His next priority group was to gain new customers. He made a list of the activities he typically performed that generated new business. He prioritized that list so if more than one project was going on he knew which task took precedence. His third group of priorities was administrative tasks. He made a list of the activities he typically performed that pertained to business administration. He prioritized them. At the end of each business day Edwin would list the tasks that needed to be done. He would run each task past his hierarchy of priorities and give it a priority according to his pre-determined hierarchy. He was no longer swayed by pressures or interest. He could now easily reach his business goals because he was always working on the tasks that were the most important.

David was the owner and manager of a small insurance office. His hierarchy of priorities that he provided for his commercial division staff looked something like this:

A. Servicing current clients

- Additional new coverage to existing clients
- Evidence of insurance or certificate of insurance
- Handling payment issues
- Responding to a VIP client
- Handling requests from management other than the above listed items.
- Reporting claims

B. Gaining New Business / Commercial Policies

- Gather quote information
- Quote / rate policies if possible
- Contact companies for review and availability
- Complete applications / supplementals / submit
- Follow up
- Present quotation
- Complete necessary paperwork and financing

C. Administrative

- Mail
- Notices from insurance companies
- Files/ filing
- Resumes
- Problems – claim, coverage
- People
- Marketing pieces development
- Agency management – administration

David had nine people on his staff. Providing this hierarchy of priorities to the staff ensured that everyone was working on the most important issues at all times.

The last practice that will help you be more effective in your prioritizing is to prioritize interruptions as soon as they come into your day. Interruptions flow into an executive's workday all day long in the form of telephone calls, emails, co-workers, customers, family, meetings etc. Eliminate as many interruptions as you can by asking yourself, Can I discard this? Can I delegate this? Can I handle this in 60 seconds or less? If you can discard, delegate, or handle the interruption in less than a minute than do so. If the interruption is one that you can not discard, delegate, or handle immediately than ask yourself one final important question. "Is this interruption more important than what I'm currently working on or is what I am currently working on more important than this interruption?" Check your hierarchy of priorities to determine which is most important and act accordingly. If what you are currently working on is more important than the interruption you can say something like this to the person interrupting you. "Carl, I really want to help you with that but I have my back up against a wall on a project. Would it be all right if I helped you with that as soon as I'm finished with this? Let the person see you write it down to get back to them. Than continue with what you were working on.

In review there are four layers to effective prioritizing. Layer one is to develop your master vision of what you want your career to be about. Determine your destiny. Layer two is to establish a hierarchy of priorities for the tasks you regularly perform. Layer three is at the end of each day look at the tasks that still need to be done and run them past your hierarchy of priorities to determine the top priorities for the following day. Finally, layer four is to assess interruptions as they come into your day and prioritize which is most important- the interruption or what you are already working on.

By prioritizing effectively you spend your time wisely. By spending your time wisely you improve your productivity. By improving your productivity you thrive in business. The first priority is to prioritize.

Visit www.OrganizeEnterprise.com
to subscribe to this newsletter.

Act on your priorities

The final phase is the Act phase. This is where you come into the office the next day. You pull the first follow-up form out of your day's file and go to work on it. You work on that until it is complete for today. You open your desk drawer and pull out the follow-up form in the front of 'today's' file and go to work on that until it is complete for the day. You continue this process all day long until the end of the day when it is time to pull out tomorrow's file and prioritize what you are going to do tomorrow.

As interruptions come to you, ask yourself if you can handle each one in 60 seconds or less. If it is going to take more than 60 seconds, ask yourself the all-important question: "Is what I'm working on more important than this interruption, or is this interruption more important than what I am currently working on?"

If what you are working on is more important than the interruption, tell the interruption that you are in the middle of something and that you will have to get back to them on a date and time you have decided. Write it on a follow-up form and enter it into the appropriate dated file in your work processing system. If you are getting back to them on the same day, put it in the proper place in your work processing system according to its priority.

If the interruption is more important than what you are working on, gather up what you are working on and put it in the front of your day's work processing system file so it will be the next priority once the interruption has been handled. You always want your desk clear except for the project you are currently working on. That way you can laser your focus on one project at a time and expedite how many projects you are able to accomplish in your day.

This is a processing system. It is not a storage system. Work flows in and goes through the process of gathering, filtering, prioritizing and acting. Work goes out. Everything needs to be entered into the processing system.

Mastery of skills

I offer you a warning. What is probably going to happen is that you will have more follow-up forms in your day's file than you can get done in a day; so you'll push it back to another day. After doing this for several days, your files become very thick. Do not make the mistake of thinking that it means this system doesn't work for you. What it means is that the system is doing exactly what it is supposed to be doing by giving you a visual, tangible representation that you still need to master the skills of discarding, delegating, and streamlining. This way, you can get it done is less time by prioritizing, acting etc. Along with following the tickler system, you need to constantly be working on mastering these skills. As you master these skills, the amount of papers in your day's file and the amount of time you have in a day will become a perfect match. In a manner of speaking you will have mastered the ability to stack and compress your Duplos.

Make your system portable

If you are using a paper-based tickler file in your desk drawer, you can create a tickler-system binder to transport the tickler-system files, thus making them portable. This binder can also serve as your planner. The binder should contain a calendar page for each month of the year. You will use this to write in appointments. The binder should also contain five folders, labeled:

- Monday
- Tuesday
- Wednesday
- Thursday
- Friday

Now you can use a paper-based calendar and carry your tickler-system file with you wherever you go. You can add forms into upcoming days even while you are away from the office, or you can store forms in the back of the binder to be added to your desk system once you return to the office.

Part III

Second Stage: Boost Your Concentration by Eliminating Distractions

3

E.N.D. C.H.A.O.S.

Twenty years ago I was not very organized. I certainly couldn't tell anyone else how to get organized. Twenty years ago I believed that highly organized people were obsessive compulsive and they were the one with the problem, not me. It wasn't until I realized how difficult I was making my life by staying disorganized that I made the commitment to get organized. I made it my life study. I focused my studies on what would improve performance and would reduce work related stress. I needed to learn what measures I could take that would improve the quality of my life and boost my personal productivity. I read over 75 organizing books, attended dozens of classes, practiced on several close family members and their offices. I found my systems worked for people who normally struggle to get organized. I eventually became a professional organizer. I became a member of the National Association of Professional Organizers and I received extensive training through that organization. I am now the past president of the Utah Association of Professional Organizers. I now train other people how to be a professional organizer and run a successful organizing business. All along my journey I looked for methods that caused things to STAY organized. I looked for methods that helped a person function on automatic pilot so they could concentrate on their project rather than the process.

I still believe there are some people who take it too far. Occasionally I'll look at my recommendations and ask myself, "Wait a minute have I taken it too far?" If it improves your ability to function and boosts your level of productivity I'm all for it. If it is just for the sake of being organized but serves no other purpose I throw it out. All of my recommendations are strategies I have discovered that truly make a difference. Having a clutter-free and organized work environment truly makes a difference.

A major source of distraction is clutter. The best way to eliminate distractions is to eliminate the clutter.

Clutter in your environment

During the second stage of getting organized, you want to create an environment that is clutter-free. Clear your desk of everything except for the single project you are working on at the moment. Everything else is a distraction. You want your files and desk drawers to be uncluttered and extremely organized. Cluttered drawers act as a substantial distraction. They make it impossible to progress on the project at hand without having to stop and look for items you need. Thick, disorderly files interfere with your work. You won't trust that you will be able to find papers you need if you file them away. As a result, you will leave papers out, causing more distractions. If you have your drawers and files so well organized that you can go on automatic pilot, they will distract you less and allow you to concentrate better. You can retrieve and return everything without having to look for it. Items are always in the exact same place every single time.

Clutter in your mind

I'm not a proponent of multi-tasking. Multi-tasking causes constant clutter in your mind. I am a strong believer in singular tasking. Singular tasking allows you to narrow your activity to just one thing at a time. Now you can easily achieve your desired result. You can do it in very little time. Then you can move onto your next task and achieve your desired result in very little time and so on and so forth. Have you ever had thoughts of what you need to remember to do float into your mind? That's clutter.

Clutter in your schedule

Have you ever completed a day's work and, upon looking back, felt like you got nothing accomplished? Your day was filled with "clutter" activities. Things that really weren't that necessary or that could have been handled in much less time, checking your email for the 100th time or waiting for someone to arrive for a meeting. If you are not careful, you could waste a lot of time filling your schedule with clutter activities. Those activities are just like the clutter on your desk. You must be quick to discard, delegate, streamline or put it away. To streamline means to handle something in very little time. Every time you are interrupted, or you move from one task to the next, or schedule an appointment, or consider your activities, ask yourself a question. Ask yourself, "Can I discard this? Can I delegate it to someone else? Can I do this in less time? Can I put this activity away all together?" Clear out the clutter from your schedule. Clear out the clutter from all your activity. It's destroying your ability to concentrate your efforts and produce maximum results.

Seven Steps to Organizing your Office

There are seven steps in the organizing process which will leave you clutter-free. Most people try to short cut the process by only doing three steps: sorting through their things, deciding where to put things, and putting them into a container. Doing all seven steps causes your space to stay organized for seven years instead of just seven hours. As I explain the steps to you, you will see how each step contributes to making the organization last. There are only seven steps and there are *always* seven steps.

It is important that you do the steps in the right order. Each step alters what needs to be done in the subsequent steps. If you do them in the wrong order, you will end up doing the wrong things. For example; if you purchase a container before you sort through your things and get rid of what needs to go, you will end up with the wrong size of container. You'll have to do the step of purchasing a container again. If you decide where to put things without first examining your situation by studying your habits, needs, and priorities, you will put things in the wrong place. You'll have to do the step where you assign the homes for things all over again.

Organize Your Office for Success

It is also important that you complete each step before moving on, to the next step. If you don't, you will end up working in circles, not really making progress or accomplishing anything. You just move stuff from place to place. I have seen people start sorting in this manner. When they came to an item that belonged in the room where they were working, they stopped sorting and, instead, started deciding where to put things. Then, without meaning to, they stopped deciding where to put things and started making a list of what containers they needed. Then they went back to their sorting activity. Since they hadn't completed the sorting before deciding where things belonged, they put things in temporary "homes." Since they made a container list before they finished sorting, they planned for the wrong size and type of container. They continually had to re-do everything and made very little progress. Without realizing it, they were moving things from point A, to point B, to point C, but they were not making any real progress. They were just moving stuff. You have heard the phrase, "The shortest distance between two points is a straight line." It is the same with organizing. The most direct route to getting your office organized is to complete each step before moving on to the next.

To help you remember the steps in order, I have created the acronym, "E.N.D. C.H.A.O.S."

E xamine Your Situation

a*N*d

D esign a Plan that Works for Your Unique Situation

C ategorize Your Things

H aul Them to Their New Destinations

A ssign the Right Home

O btain the Right Container

S ustain Your Systems Daily

Now, the objective is to END CHAOS in your office. However, most people begin to organize by diving into the categorizing process, leaving out the Examine and Design (END) steps. Without END you are simply left with CHAOS, which is exactly what happens to the space you've organized in about four weeks. By taking the time to properly examine your situation and design a plan that will work best for *your* situation, you end up with an organized office that *stays* organized.

For a free download of our special report "25 Quick Tips to Finally Get Control of Your Messy Environment" visit: www.OrganizeEnterprise.com/25quicktips.

4

Why Do You Want to Get Organized?

The E in END CHAOS stands for Examine Your Situation. This is the first step in the organizing process. Closely examining your situation will help you make distinctions that will alter the way you organize. Those alterations will produce a different result. That different result will affect how well your office stays organized. So, how effective you are in your examination impacts how well your office will stay organized.

A complete examination consists of four different areas of discovery.

1)   discover why you want to get organized.

2)   discover what is already happening.

3)   discover what you want to have happen.

4)   discover what's causing the disorganization in your office.

There are a number of things you should consider while examining your situation. They are listed and numbered here along with brief explanations of what you are really trying to determine.

Why do you want to get organized? Consider the costs/benefits

Sorting through your stuff and getting rid of things you've been hanging onto can be painful. If you are not clear about why you are doing it, you are not going to do it: at least, you won't do it thoroughly. Getting all the stuff in your office organized is a lot of work. You are not going to see it through unless you have a good enough reason <u>why</u>!

Recognize what disorganization has cost you in the past, what it is costing you now, and what it is going to cost you in the future. Explore what it costs you socially, financially, physically, mentally, and spiritually. Explore what it is going to cost you 1 year, 5 years, 10 years, even 20 years from now if you don't learn to be better organized.

Once you have associated enough pain to having a disorganized office and enough pleasure to getting and keeping an organized office, you will be motivated to do whatever it takes to get your office organized and keep it that way.

EXERCISE:

WHY DO YOU WANT TO GET ORGANIZED?

_____

_____

_____

_____

_____

_____

_____

For a free download of our special report "25 Quick Tips to Finally Get Control of Your Messy Environment" visit: www.OrganizeEnterprise.com/25quicktips.

5

What is Happening?

What areas appear to be fairly well organized?

What are the logical reasons those areas have stayed organized?

Look over surfaces; open drawers; look through binders, containers, niches, etc. The answers to these questions will help you identify what your organizing style is. We all know that people have their own learning style. Some learn best visually; others, auditorally; and still others, kinesthetically. It doesn't mean they can't learn something using the other modalities; it just means that one modality is their dominant style of learning and that it's easier for them to learn *using* that modality.

What isn't as commonly known is that every person has his or her own organizing style—a way of keeping things organized that comes more easily for them. It doesn't mean that all the principles of organizing don't apply. It just means that people are better organizers using one style over another.

To determine your organizing style, look through your office. Without considering your history or the truth behind the matter, look at what *appears* to be fairly well organized. Find 6 things and list them across the top of a page.

After you identify a number of places that appear to be relatively well organized, take a good look at them and ask yourself, "What are the logical reasons that they have stayed organized?" Some possible answers might be:

Organize Your Office for Success

- It stays organized because we have developed the habit of keeping that organized.

-. The container is a good fit for the items that go there.

- The area is well lit and therefore, comfortable to work in.

- Items are stored at a convenient location.

- It stays organized because it is as easy to put items away as it is to leave them out.

- Items have clearly defined and obvious homes.

- You straighten the area every day, etc...

List the reasons why each organized location stays organized. Write the reasons in a vertical list underneath each of the six items you listed at the top of the column.

1.	2.	3.	4.	5.	6.

Now, compare those lists. See if different organized locations have logical reasons in common. Did convenience of location apply to more than one place? What about the area being well lit as a common reason? Find the reasons that have the greatest frequency, and that will show you what your organizing style is.

After you know what seems to work for you, you will want to implement that style throughout the office, as much as possible.

For example, if the logical reasons prove to be "the area is at a convenient location," "it is well lit," and "everybody knows where the items belong," then make sure that everything throughout your office is at the most convenient location. Also, make sure your office is very well lit and is thoroughly labeled so everybody knows where things belong.

3) What are your habits?

Now look at what your habits and tendencies are. A common mistake people make when organizing their office is that they organize their things a certain way then say, "From now on, I am going to . . ." They set up their organization to remain intact only if they develop a new habit. Habits are difficult to develop. The chances of them developing new habits are slim. When you are organizing your office, you want to require yourself to develop as few new habits as possible. Rather, look at the habits you already have and then organize around those existing habits.

Some examples are as follows:

Steven had the habit of leaving all the paperwork out on his desk (actually, it covered all of his surfaces) until the project was complete and ready to be filed away in storage. Although he had papers strewn all over his desk, he had the habit of returning the books to the bookcase (which was in a very convenient location) as soon as he was done looking at them. So, we combined his habits of leaving papers horizontal and putting books away in the bookshelf by clearing out one or two book shelves and making a "home" for papers to be stacked neatly on the shelves until they were ready to be filed. His desk was clear and his office organized by working with habits that he already had.

Organize Your Office for Success

Maria had the habit of writing everything down on post-it notes and plastering them over all the surfaces. We simply gave a "home" for the post-it notes in a 10" x 10" space. As soon as it was covered, old notes had to come off to make room for the new notes. She kept her habit of writing on the post-it notes and sticking them on a surface. We simply defined some limits so she would know when it was time to take some post-it notes down. The 10" x 10" space kept the mess to a minimum, but she could still have the visual reminders that the post-it notes provided.

Jasmine had the habit of stacking on her desk packs of papers that needed her to take some action before passing them on. There was no room to work at her desk. It was covered with "take action" piles. We simply set up a work processing system for her. She knew where to look to see what else she needed to do; her desk remained clear and she was able to complete her work.

Bill had piles of paper all over his office. As we examined his situation, it took a little time to determine exactly what his habits were. Finally, I recognized that the piles of paper were there because Bill had the habit of procrastinating making decisions as to what to do with paper. He didn't lay papers down because he didn't

---

EXERCISE:

WHAT ARE YOUR HABITS?

_____

_____

_____

_____

_____

_____

_____

_____

---

have *time* to deal with them or put them away. He laid them down because he didn't want to have to make the necessary *decisions* on *what* to do with them. We simply set up a work processing system in his desk drawer. Every paper that came into his office immediately went into his work processing system. This worked with Bills habits by setting in place a needed tool to keep the process of paper flowing.

A key ingredient to a well-organized office is to work with your habits. Don't fight them.

To discover your habits and tendencies, look to the piles and messes around your office. Ask yourself "What are these papers?" "How did this (paper) get here?" "What happened here to create that pile?" "What habits contributed to it?" Ask these questions enough, and behavior patterns will begin to surface. You'll be able to objectively determine what your habits are.

Ascertaining your habits and designing a customized plan to work with your habits is a skill you will develop over time. You will discover obvious habits. Underlying, recurring habits will surface. Then, when you design your plan, ask yourself, "How can I best organize my space so that I am able to work with that habit?" Answers will come to you.

4) Name the 20% of your things in this space that you are using in your current life.

5) If there was a fire in your office and you only had 10 minutes to save your most important possessions and papers, which would they be?

6) What are the items you see that bring you a lot of joy?

Organizing your office in a manner that will stay organized is going to require you to **eliminate everything you are not using on a regular basis** and use the space to provide adequate homes for the things you *are* using.

Drake had his file drawers full and his surfaces covered with documents from past projects or communications. He needed to clear out all the paperwork pertaining to work he was no longer working on in order to make room for all the paperwork that pertained to the work he was currently working on. He had his desk drawers full of odds and ends that had been stashed there over time but he was not really using them for anything. Drake needed to clean out his drawers of all the items that he was not using at least once a month in his current life. Drake's bookshelves were loaded with books he was no longer referring to. He needed to clear out the books he was not using in order to provide adequate space for the books he was referring to all the time.

What are you actually using? The 80/20 rule states that out of all your possessions, you only use about 20%. The other 80% are things you *used* to use, things you feel you *should* be using or *should* hang onto, or things you think you *might* use some day.

The problem occurs when you try to keep these things. Since you're not actively using them, you put them in the back of your files and drawers. Those become full, so you find yourself putting them on the top of your desk, filing cabinet, and shelves. Those spaces become full, so you put them on the chairs, windowsill, or floor. Little by little your used-to(s), should(s), and might(s) squeeze you right out of your office. It's all being used for storage.

a)   Do you have things in your office left over from old projects?

b)   Is your filing cabinet full of old files?

c)   Do you have paperwork that serves no purpose, but since someone made that copy and gave it to you, you feel like you should hang onto it?

d)   Do you put a lot of effort into something in the past? Eventually, you didn't want to use it anymore, but since you spent good time and money on it, you feel like you should hang onto it.

e)   Do you have reference books you're not using or magazines that you're not finding time to read?

> EXERCISE:
>
> NAME THE 20% OF YOUR THINGS YOU ARE USING IN
> YOUR CURRENT LIFE:
>
> _____
>
> _____
>
> _____
>
> _____
>
> _____
>
> _____

Look through your office, including the drawers, and list the items you are using in your current work. It is not necessary to go over the entire office. Do this exercise for five to ten minutes so as to mentally prepare yourself for getting rid of a lot of stuff. You want to say it out loud because doing so helps you to recognize that you have a lot of stuff you don't really need and should get rid of.

You have a simple choice. Either you can use your office as a place to function and thrive in, or you can use it as a storage facility. You can't have it both ways. One squeezes out the other so you are left with one by default. Get rid of all that excess!

This exercise helps you recognize how ridiculous it is to have your office filled with stuff you are not even using. Verbalize the items you use on a regular basis. Doing this before you start the sorting process will help you make better decisions about what to keep and what to get rid of. Getting rid of your used to(s), should(s) and might(s) will help you make substantial progress in your quest for an organized office.

**For a free download of our special report
"25 Quick Tips to Finally Get Control of
Your Messy Environment" visit:
www.OrganizeEnterprise.com/25quicktips.**

6

What Do You Want to Have Happen?

hat would you like the end result to be?

Drake wanted his office space organized. The three things he must have accomplished was having all the cluttered surfaces cleared off, have an organized filing system set up, and have a way to process his incoming paperwork so it didn't pile up in his office. The thing that needed to be fixed or improved the most was a way to process the incoming paperwork so it didn't pile up in his office.

You need to establish in the beginning what you want created by the end so all your efforts move you toward that target. The above questions help you zoom in from broad, general outcomes to three specific outcomes and finally, to the single, most important outcome. This helps you know what you need to accomplish above everything else.

EXERCISE:

WHAT WOULD YOU LIKE THE END RESULT TO BE?

a) HOW WOULD THINGS BE DIFFERENT AT THE CONCLUSION OF THE PROJECT FROM THE WAY THEY ARE NOW?

_____

_____

b) IDEALLY, WHAT THREE THINGS MUST BE ACCOMPLISHED?

_____

_____

_____

c) WHAT MUST BE CHANGED, FIXED, OR IMPROVED THE MOST?

_____

_____

_____

2) What needs to be better organized?

Clarify what you want to be organized better. You will probably have a number of things that need to be organized. Establish a hierarchy of your priorities. List everything that frustrates you. You want to address all the issues. When you organize an office and leave a few things disorganized, they spill over onto the things you did organize and cause your organization to unravel. Make this list as detailed and complete as you can. Look closely at your things to stimulate your thinking about the list. Then, when you design your plan, you can include solutions to deal with these issues.

Organize Your Office for Success

WHAT NEEDS TO BE BETTER ORGANIZED?

_____

_____

_____

_____

_____

_____

_____

Drake made a list of what needed to be better organized. His list included the following:

- Surfaces need to be cleared of clutter.

- Filing system needs to be made simple.

- Drawers need to be organized so he can find things.

- A process system for incoming work so it gets handled immediately.

- Training on how to more effectively work with his administrative assistant.

- Electronic organizing so he can find documents quickly.

- A structured schedule created so he wastes less time.

- A paper based contact management system.

- A method of delegation that didn't allow things to fall between the cracks.

- Training on how to efficiently handle interruptions.

- A meeting agenda that helped meetings take less time.

3) What are your long-term and short-term goals in your business/life?

EXERCISE:

WHAT WOULD YOU LIKE THE END RESULT TO BE?

a) WHAT ARE YOUR LONG-TERM AND SHORT-TERM GOALS IN YOUR BUSINESS/LIFE?

_____

_____

_____

b) WHAT ITEMS ARE THE MOST ESSENTIAL IN HELPING YOU REACH YOUR GOALS?

_____

_____

_____

_____

_____

---

4) What items are the most essential in helping you reach your goals?

Get clear on what you want for yourself, your business, and your office. This way, when you are finished organizing your office, each area will end up contributing to an environment that supports you in obtaining your most important outcomes.

What are your long-term goals? Imagine yourself 65 years old, sitting alone in your office. You're reflecting on your career, recognizing it's almost over, and you're asking yourself, *Did I accomplish the things I most needed to accomplish? Did I experience the things I most wanted to experience?* What would those accomplishments and experiences be? After you determine that, ask yourself, *What items in my office do I want to have highly accessible so I can achieve those accomplishments and experiences?*

What are your short-term goals? What do you want to excel in, right now in your current work? What do you want to accomplish and experience over the next year? What items do you need accessible to accomplish those goals?

Working off the list of what is most important to you helps you to know what things you need to provide a good home for.

When I'm doing a Needs Assessment with a client, it never fails that when we come to the questions about their goals and what they value, they look at me questioningly and ask, "Why do you need to know that to organize my desk?" A good example of this comes from a client I consulted with who had his office set up to process papers. Yet, when we went through his goals and highest priorities, we found that the most important purpose for his office was to meet and interact with people. So, we organized his office to meet that need first and paper processing second. He tells me that he has been on the fast track to accomplishing his career goals ever since.

5) What activities do you want to do in your office?

6) What items are needed for the activities you want to do in this space?

7) What are your main responsibilities at work?

Once you establish the activities you want to do in your office, you need to find out what supplies and containers are needed for these activities. Then you'll need to break the office down into four or five smaller regions. The regions may overlap each other. A region is the place where a certain activity takes place and where all the supplies for that activity are stored. The goal is to create a cockpit scenario where you can reach everything you need without doing any traveling while in your region/work station. For example:

Region #1

Region	*Supplies*	*Containers*
Computer	Computer	Desk or Stand
	Keyboard	CD / Disk Organizer
	Mouse	Cable Organizer
	CPU	Shelves for Manuals
	Monitor	
	Mouse Pad	
	Disks	
	CD's	
	Manuals	
	Cables	
	Accessories	

You will want to arrange all supplies and containers to be within arm's reach, so you don't have to travel while you're sitting in front of the computer.

EXERCISE:

CREATE THE TABLE FOR YOUR FIRST REGION

Region #1

Region	**Supplies**	**Containers**

Organize Your Office for Success

Region #2

Region	Supplies	Containers
Telephone	Telephone	Phone Book Organizer
	Phone Books	Contact Organizer
	Contact Information	
	Accessories	Desk
	Rolodex cards	Rolodex
	Communication Logs	Chair
	Phone Lists	Drawers
	Pens	Hanging Files
	Business Cards	

You will want to arrange all supplies and containers to be within arm's reach so you don't have to travel while you're talking on the telephone.

EXERCISE:

CREATE THE TABLE FOR YOUR SECOND REGION

Region #2

Region	Supplies	Containers

Region #3

Region	Supplies	Containers
Meetings	Table Desk Chairs Files / Agendas Whiteboard Pens Notepads	Files

You will want to arrange all supplies and containers to be within arm's reach so you don't have to travel while you and your guests are meeting around the desk or table.

EXERCISE:

CREATE THE TABLE FOR YOUR THIRD REGION

Region #3

Region	Supplies	Containers

Region #4

Region	Supplies	Containers
Paperwork / Work	Files	Desk
	Work Processing System	Hanging Files
	Light	File Folders
	Pen	Labels
	Papers to be Filed	Trash Can
		Recycle Bin
		Shredder
		Filing Cabinet
		File Pockets
		File Racks
		Tabs

You will want to arrange all supplies and containers to be within arm's reach so you don't have to travel while you're doing paperwork at your desk.

EXERCISE:

CREATE THE TABLE FOR YOUR FOURTH REGION

Region #4

Region	Supplies	Containers

Organize Your Office for Success

<u>**Region #5**</u>

Region	Supplies	Containers
Reference	Books	Shelves
	Reference Files	File Cabinet
	Newsletters	Computer
	Internet	
	Binders	
	Magazines	
	Reports	

You will want to arrange all supplies and containers to be within arm's reach so you don't have to travel while sitting in the chair you study your reference information in.

EXERCISE:
CREATE THE TABLE FOR YOUR FIFTH REGION

Region #5

Region	Supplies	Containers

7

What is Causing the Disorganization?

A nybody can tidy up a drawer. But, if you don't address what was causing it to be disorganized in the first place, it's just going to get messed up again.

The next several questions help you to determine the cause of the disorganization.

1) What is causing the disorganization?

EXERCISE:

WHAT IS CAUSING THE DISORGANIZATION?

_____

_____

_____

_____

_____

2) Is access to your storage hampered in some way? How so?

This is where you explore how easy or difficult it is for you to put things away properly. Are items stored at the place they are first used so traveling is not required to put it away? Is it easier to put it away than it is to get it out? Can you eliminate any motions in the putting away process? Is there a proper fit between your items and the containers and spaces you have designated to store the items? These are all questions you need to ask yourself when determining if access to your storage is hampered some way.

EXERCISE:

IS ACCESS TO YOUR STORAGE HAMPERED IN SOME WAY AND HOW SO?

_____

_____

_____

_____

_____

_____

_____

3) Do you have ways to expand your storage space? What are they?

If your closets, drawers, and files are full, you'll have all your surfaces covered with stuff and no way to keep it organized. People often try to cram too many pieces of furniture or large storage containers into an office space. Then they cram too much stuff into the furniture. One principle of organization says: there must be a proper fit. Having a proper fit is a primary requirement for having your things **stay** organized. If you have more stuff than you have space, you have three choices for how to fix it:

1)   Eliminate stuff,

2)   Expand your storage capacity, or

3)   Make the best use of every inch of storage space.

EXERCISE:

DO YOU HAVE WAYS TO EXPAND YOUR STORAGE SPACE? WHAT ARE THEY?

_____

_____

_____

_____

_____

_____

_____

_____

_____

Here are a couple of examples:

Shawn's business had floor-to-ceiling paperwork. Because of legal issues, he could not simply eliminate the paperwork. He rented an off-site storage facility to house his archive files. This allowed a proper fit inside his business offices.

Deborah was in sales. Her office was overcrowded with client's files, inventory of her products, and promotional materials. It was material she was currently using. She didn't have the funds to rent an off-site storage facility, so we simply built shelves from floor to ceiling on three of her office walls. She put the most commonly used items in the most convenient locations and the least frequently used items in the hard-to-reach locations. Everything was highly accessible and well preserved, and she was able to function at her very best.

While you are examining your situation, determine which combination of the three solutions you will need to implement to get things back to where there is a proper fit. This can be from the size of the room all the way to the number of papers in a file folder.

4) Do you leave things out as a visual reminder of what you have to do?

As a rule, move toward using a tickler system to put things out of sight but in a location you will be sure to see in order to remind you of what you need to do.

Using a tickler system helps you keep a reality check on how many projects you can get around to. Discard or delegate some projects to make your to-do list more realistic. Streamline or simplify your tasks. Having all your tasks stored in daily files helps you see how unrealistic it is for you to get around to all those tasks yourself.

EXERCISE:

DO YOU LEAVE THINGS OUT AS A VISUAL REMINDER OF WHAT YOU HAVE TO DO?

5) Do you prefer things out where you can see them, or do you prefer things stored out of sight so your surfaces are clear, etc.?

Do not try to make yourself keep your paper filed neatly in your file cabinet if that is contrary to what you prefer. Decide what you prefer and design a plan that works with your preference. It is foolish to set up a system that doesn't work with your preferences. You won't keep it up.

If you want to get organized, but you see some subtle benefits to being disorganized, you'll sabotage your efforts. Until you discover the causes of your disorganization (both obvious and hidden) and address them, you will not be able to organize your office in a manner that stays organized. By dealing with the deep-seated causes directly, you can free yourself from chronic disorganization that has left you in chaos most of your career. The following questions will help you determine some underlying causes. Sometimes the disorganization serves you in some way. You need to think of alternative ways to meet the needs that the clutter is meeting, so you can feel comfortable being truly organized.

EXERCISE:

DO YOU PREFER THINGS OUT WHERE YOU CAN SEE THEM OR DO YOU PREFER THINGS STORED OUT OF SIGHT SO YOUR SURFACES ARE CLEAR?

6) Do you have an unrealistic workload?

This is another cause of disorganization. You need to address this cause head on so you are able to get better organized in a manner that will stay organized.

7) Does your clutter serve you in some way?

a)   Does it make you feel needed and in demand?

Some people fear not having enough stuff surrounding them. They'll not necessarily need the nicest of things, but they need a greater number of them. They need plenty of everything in order to feel safe, secure, and comfortable. Some people keep their office a mess in order to feel like they are actively involved in important projects. Others keep a lot of clutter in their office to help them feel like they are valued or in high demand.

b)   Does it hide you from things you don't want to do?

Some people hide from the discovery of being a success or failure. They hide socially from issues or tasks they don't want to have to think about. They should deal with the real issues directly. Then they won't need to rely on chaos to protect them.

c)   Does the clutter make you feel important because you are too important to do the "cleaning up?"

Some people leave the clutter out as a reminder of their importance. They feel like they are too important to have to clean up and the messy clutter reminds them of how important they are.

d)   Does the clutter make you feel safe?

Some people use clutter as a security blanket. A comforter if you will. They feel like the clutter validates that they are needed or in demand. That it represents job security. The problem with that belief is that often the opposite is closer to the truth. The clutter irritates the boss or customer and threatens their position with the company.

EXERCISE:

DOES YOUR CLUTTER SERVE YOU SOME WAY?

_____

_____

_____

_____

_____

_____

_____

_____

_____

_____

_____

---

8) Does the idea of getting rid of a lot of the things in your space fill you with anxiety and dread?

Some people attach sentimental value to non-living things. Do you have things in your office that represent successes you have had in the past? Are you afraid of getting rid of those things, believing that you will lose the respect or honor of the past?

a) What about things filling your mind?

Some people find comfort in having their mind busy and full. They feel anxious or bored if there is not a lot to think about.

b) What about things filling your schedule? Some people find comfort in being busy with appointments to keep, projects to work on, and accomplishments to pursue. Free time may make some people anxious.

EXERCISE:

DOES THE IDEA OF GETTING RID OF A LOT OF THINGS IN YOUR
SPACE, MIND, OR SCHEDULE FILL YOU WITH ANXIETY AND DREAD?

_____

_____

_____

_____

_____

_____

_____

**For a free download of our special report
"25 Quick Tips to Finally Get Control of
Your Messy Environment" visit:
www.OrganizeEnterprise.com/25quicktips.**

8

Design Your Plan

After you make a thorough examination of your situation, you are ready to move on to step number two, which is to design a plan that will work for your unique situation. **The N and D in END CHAOS stand for aNd Design a plan that will work for your unique situation. This is the second step in the organizing process.**

This is the step in the organizing process where you take the information you discovered in your examination and use it to shape the environment in your office. There are many things to consider when designing your master plan.

Design with your target(s) in mind

When you sit down to design a plan the first thing you want to do is look at your business goals over the next 1, 10, 20 years and make sure the activities you wanted to take place in your office are in line with your goals and desired outcomes.

Create cockpits for workstations

In the following example I have outlined one office space and drawn out where the different work regions should be set up. Each diagram differs in that it assigns supplies for specific regions into drawers or spaces for that region.

You need to arrange your office furniture so it is in an L-shape or a U-shape arrangement. An L-shaped arrangement would have the desk in front of you and files and workspace down your left or right side. A U-shaped arrangement would have the desk in front of you, possibly with files and workspace or possibly with a computer stand at your left or right side and more files, cabinets, etc. directly behind you.

COMPUTER REGION

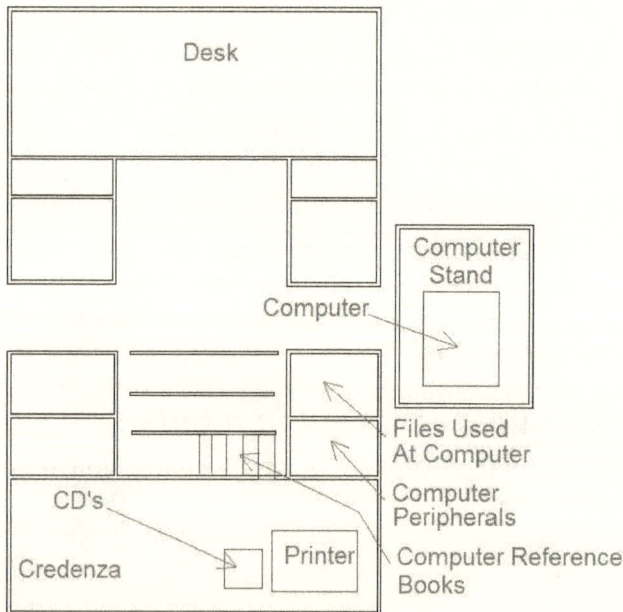

Desk

Computer
Stand

Computer

Files Used
At Computer

Computer
Peripherals

CD's

Printer

Computer Reference
Books

Credenza

Organize Your Office for Success

A computer region would have everything computer-related within arms reach of you when you are facing the computer. You may have to turn to the left or to the right but you should not have to travel. All files used at the computer should be stored in a file drawer directly next to the computer. Computer peripherals should be stored nearby. Your computer reference books should be within arms reach of the computer. This demonstration shows the printer and the CD organizer nearby as well. Everything should be within arms reach while sitting up to the computer. That is what you want to accomplish.

This example of the meeting region shows you the arrangement of the furniture to facilitate a meeting for three people. The chairs face each other. The white board is hung where all three participants of the meeting can see it and can write on it. The desk top is cleared for the meeting so the only papers on the desk are the papers pertaining to the meeting you are in. The desk drawer holds the active files which includes the meeting agendas and minutes.

MEETING REGION

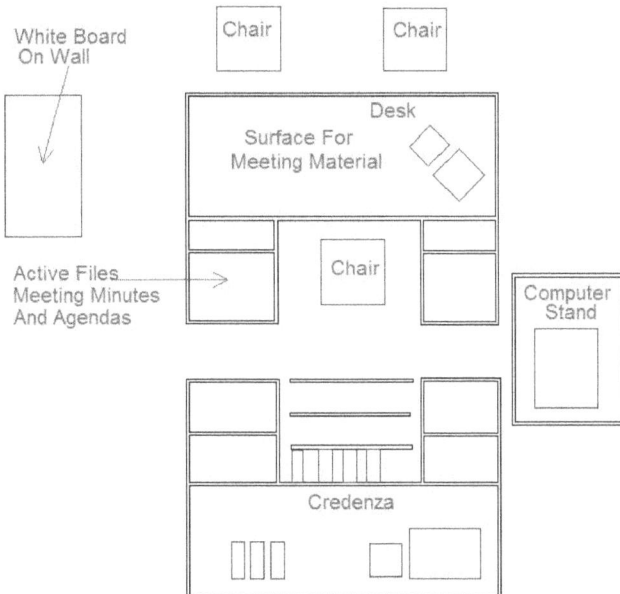

White Board On Wall

Chair

Chair

Desk

Surface For Meeting Material

Active Files Meeting Minutes And Agendas

Chair

Computer Stand

Credenza

Organize Your Office for Success

This example of the reference region shows you how easy it is to store your most active reference material within your personal desk space. Notice how the shelves for reference books are right next to the file drawer used for reference files. If you have 3-5 reference books that you are constantly referring to you may want to put them on the credenza top in a telephone book organizer of your choosing. They also should be stored near the other reference material. This way when you are looking up reference information you can find everything you need without traveling around the office or your desk space.

REFERENCE REGION

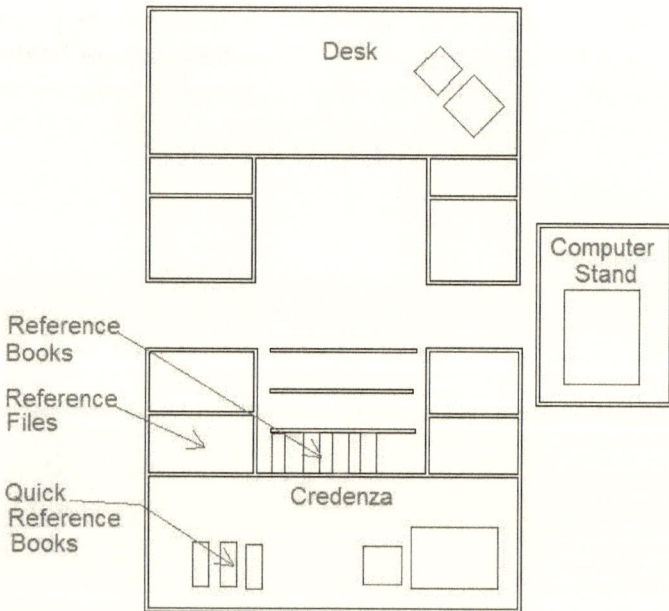

Organize Your Office for Success

This example of the paperwork region demonstrates how you can sit up to your desk and facilitate the management of paperwork by simply using the drawers to your left or to your right along with the use of your desktop. The only exception to this is the one drawer in the credenza which will require you to turn in your chair to retrieve papers from that file drawer. That is why you store the less active files in the credenza drawer. The files in the credenza drawer are less active and rarely accessed so it makes sense to store them in the credenza rather than then the desk.

PAPERWORK REGION

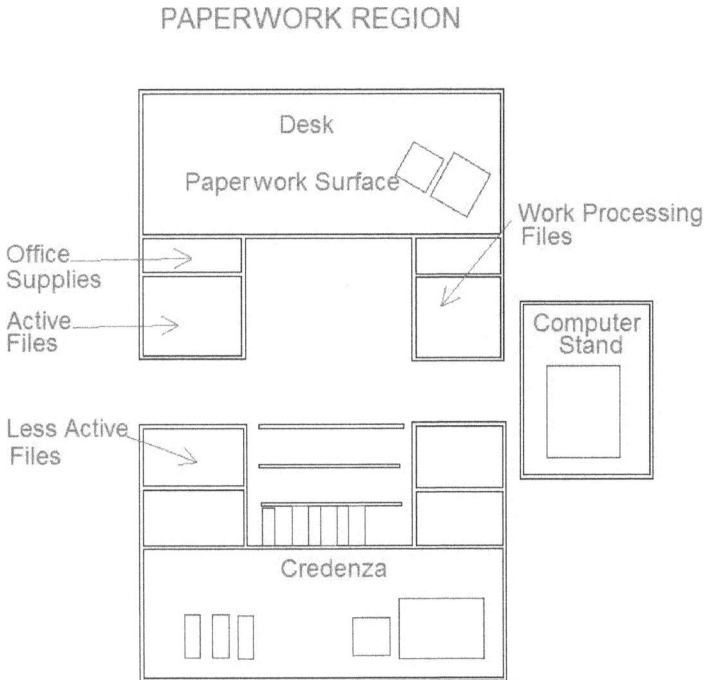

Organize Your Office for Success

The telephone region merely has the telephone, telephone books, contact information, communication log, and memo pad all stored together. This allows you to function at your best when making or receiving calls.

TELEPHONE REGION

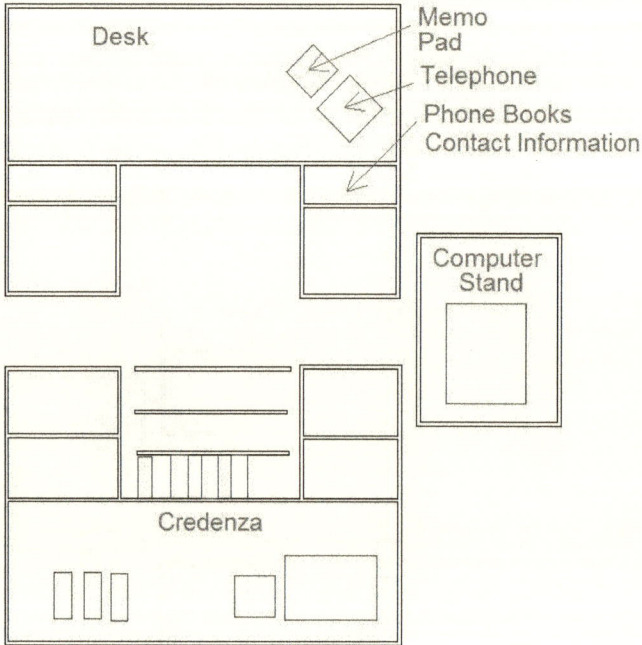

Coordinate activities, supplies, and containers

Next, refer to your needs assessment on page (?) where you have listed the regions, supplies and containers needed. Decide where in your furniture arrangement you are going to establish each region you listed. Plan out where and how to store the supplies for each region so everything is within arm's reach and so everything follows the seven strategies that minimize the maintenance.

Respond to your examination

After you have your regions established, fine tune your plan by referring to all the questions in your examination and design solutions. As you come up with ideas, run them past the seven strategies to make sure they will require the minimum amount of maintenance. The seven strategies are:

Do all 7 steps of the organizing process: Examine, Design, Categorize, Haul, Assign the Right Home, Obtain the Right Container, Sustain Your Systems Daily

Insist on a proper fit between your container and the size and number of contents you are keeping in the container.

- Store everything at the place it is first used.

- Make it easier to put away than it is to get out.

- Eliminate extra motions in the putting away process.

- Label! Label! Label!

- Maintain your systems daily.

With each examination question you review, you will add parts and pieces of your plan until the entire examination has been addressed and the entire plan has been designed.

Some of the questions in the examination are to explore psychological issues that may be impairing your organization. As a standard practice, I suggest you talk to a professional who can help you with those internal issues.

Remember, you want to insist on maintaining a proper fit. For example: papers in file folders, file folders in hanging files, or hanging files a file cabinet drawer all need to fit properly. A proper fit is about 80% of their capacity. Leave room to grow.

When designing your plan and systems, consider both the flow of items throughout the process and the flow of the people working in the space. For example: Look at the process that different types of paperwork go through while in your office space. Eliminate points of congestion and put in place what is needed so there are no breakdowns in the flow. Be sure you build an "out" door. This is a natural way for things to go out of the office in a timely manner, whether it is to the recycle bin, a co-worker, to the boss, or whatever.

A good example of the "out" door concept is Tony: Tony had a ton of paper in his office. What we discovered was that he had an "in" door (stuff comes in, stuff comes in, stuff comes in), but he didn't have any kind of an "out" door. Papers rarely went out. We simply inserted a place for paper to go out by placing a container near the door. Therefore, when he finished a project and no longer needed the paperwork, he just set it in that container with a post-it note indicating where it needed to go. He asked his secretary to watch the container and (while continuing the process flow) deliver the paper to wherever it needed to go–whether into storage, back to central filing, to a co-worker's office, or wherever.

Take notice of how you feel while in your different work regions. If you like how you feel when you're doing something, you'll do it. If you don't like how you feel while you're doing something, you won't do it (at least, you'll put it off as long as possible). Pay attention to your internal feelings when you're in your regions or doing your activities. Make needed changes so it feels better. Have fun with that.

Finally, you need to assign a time for each stage of your organizing project.

Example:

Activity	Hours	Day & Time
Categorizing morning	12 hours	Monday all day & Tuesday
Hauling	1 ½ hours	Tuesday afternoon
Assigning a Home	3 hours	Tuesday afternoon
Obtaining a Container	6 hours	Wednesday
Sustaining	10 minutes	Daily

EXERCISE:

ASSIGN A TIME FOR EACH STAGE OF YOUR ORGANIZING PROJECT

Activity	**Hours**	**Day & Time**
Categorizing		
Hauling		
Assigning a Home		
Obtaining a Container		
Sustaining		

For a free download of our special report "25 Quick Tips to Finally Get Control of Your Messy Environment" visit: www.OrganizeEnterprise.com/25quicktips.

9

Categorize Your Things & Haul Them to Their Destination

The C and H in END CHAOS stand for Categorize your things and Haul them to their destinations. These are the third and fourth steps in the organizing process.

Categorizing Paperwork

Set things up for the de-cluttering process. You will need 5 boxes, 60 hanging files, 100 manila folders, trash bags, post-it notes and a pen. Sit behind your desk like you would if you were working. You should have five boxes on the floor or on a chair next to you. Two of the boxes should have 30 hanging files in them. Inside the first few hanging files you should have manila folders labeled "Other Room," "To" (other key people in your office), "Casual Reading," and "Take Home." Have the manila file folders where you can reach them as you need them. The other three boxes should be close to where you throw away, recycle, or shred papers. Label the three boxes "Shred," "Recycle," and "Trash."

The first outcome you should pursue is getting the desk surface cleared. Pick up a paper and ask yourself the question, "Under what circumstances am I going to need this again?" If it can be recycled, toss it in the box labeled "Recycle." If it needs to be thrown away, toss it in the box labeled "Trash." If it needs to be shredded, toss it into the box labeled "Shred." If you need to do something with it other than file it away, decide what date you are going to take that action. Write that date on a manila file folder and file it in alphabetical order (or in numerical order, as the case may be) in your box of hanging files. If you don't need to do anything with a paper, but it needs to be filed for future reference, decide what heading you would like to put it under, then write that heading on a manila file folder or, where applicable, insert it into an existing file you have already created in your new system. File it in your box of hanging files in alphabetical order.

> *Your five choices are:*
> *recycle,*
> *toss,*
> *shred,*
> *date you will take care of it, and*
> *heading you want it filed under*

As necessary, you will need to bring additional paper/things to your desk to sort through, empty the recycle box, trash box and shred box as needed, and haul all paperwork to its appropriate destination.

When you come across things other than paper that need to go into another room, or have some action taken on them, or put into storage, or whatever, start piles/boxes for those destinations. These boxes will fill as you organize the office.

Organize Your Office for Success

To determine what you should keep and what you should get rid of, simply ask yourself the following questions to lead you to making better decisions. Questions such as:

1)   Under what circumstances would I need that again?

2)   Is there somewhere else I could get it if I ever did need it?

3)   Why am I hanging onto it?

4)   Have I asked my accountant/attorney/boss what I should hang onto?

a) Should I call the _____ office and ask them how long I need to hang onto this?

b) What's the worst thing that could happen if I get rid of it?

A real obstacle to having a clutter-free office is having too much junk. It might be paperwork, books, awards, binders, or any number of things. I recognize that some people have a hard time parting with their things, especially if it represents work they accomplished in the past. Yet, there is an irrefutable fact: you cannot have a clutter-free office when it is full of too much stuff. Paper is the number one culprit.

Once you finish decluttering your desktop, start clearing off the other surfaces and bringing items/papers to your desk so you can sort through them. Continue doing that until all the surfaces are clear. Then dig through any boxes, file drawers, other drawers, cabinets, shelves etc. Start at the right side of the door and go all the way around the room so you don't miss anything.

As you come to full files or binders, don't try to pass them on or put them back; be sure to look through the file/binder and see if there are any pages you can toss at this point.

Just go through paper until all of it is sorted. Then you'll set things up differently to sort through everything else in the office.

Sorting through all the paper could take several sessions. Organizing paperwork takes four times as much time as organizing other things. Just be patient. You are right on track. One file drawer represents close to 3000 pieces of paper. This means 3000 small decisions you must make. It takes time. It is exhausting work. Don't

Organize Your Office for Success

work longer than four hours. It is too tiring. You'll stop making good decisions.

Break the sorting into three segments:

1)	Paperwork – You'll do this sorting in the beginning.

2)	Everything that belongs in a drawer that is not a file drawer – You'll do this sorting after you have finished sorting the paperwork.

3)	Everything that does not belong in a drawer – You'll do this sorting as your final sorting phase.

Categorizing Electronic Documents

Categorize electronic files much like you categorized the paper files. Whenever possible, you want to use the same folder headings that you used in the paper file folders.

1)	Look through every document and decide if it can be deleted, forwarded to someone else, renamed, or put into a folder with an appropriate heading.

2)	After you have looked through every document, look through every folder for any contents that can now be deleted, forwarded, renamed or put into a different folder.

3)	When you are done with the categorizing step you should have all electronic documents inside an electronic folder. You want broader categories with fewer folders. They should be named and in alphabetical order. When possible they should be named the same (word for word) as your paper file folders. This simplifies the filing and retrieving process.

4)	De-clutter email by first doing your Inbox and then go through all your email folders. Sort through and decide what can be deleted, forwarded, renamed, or put in different folders. When you are done, double check to see if any folders can be combined so there will be fewer folders and if they all have accurate headings. This should really streamline your emails.

Categorizing (Non-File) Drawer Items

The following is the step-by-step process you'll use to sort through the things that belong in a drawer other than a file drawer.

1)   Set up four boxes. Have them labeled "Daily," "Weekly," "Monthly," and "Less than Monthly."

2)   Look through your office for anything you are going to want kept in a drawer (other than a file drawer). Put each of those things in the boxes based on how frequently they are used. Toss or take home items you are not using on a regular basis.

3)   The drawers should be empty at this point. Everything should be in the boxes. You should have also checked all cabinets, shelves, surfaces, etc. for items you will want kept in a drawer.

4)   When you sort through everything other than paper, you are going to need to set up a few extra boxes for "Storage Room," "Other Room," "Take Home," and any other destinations you come up with.

Categorizing (Non-Drawer) Items

Finally, sort through everything in the office that is not going to end up in a drawer. Use the boxes you have for "Trash," "Goodwill," "Storage Room," "Other Room," and "Take Home" as you need them.

**For a free download of our special report
"25 Quick Tips to Finally Get Control of
Your Messy Environment" visit:
www.OrganizeEnterprise.com/25quicktips.**

10

Assign the Right Home for Everything

The A in END CHAOS stands for Assign the Right Home. This is the fifth step in the organizing process. You need to *assign* a home for everything. Assigning your things to the right home will help you function at your very best and keep your maintenance to a minimum.

Assigning Homes for Paperwork

You already made preliminary files when you sorted through your paper, created a manila file folder, and filed them alphabetically in your hanging file boxes. Now it's time to arrange your files how they will be in the finished filing system.

The rules of a good filing system are as follows:

• Maintain fewer files with broader headings.

It's better to have 20 files with 40 pieces of paper in each file than it is to have 80 files with 10 pieces of paper in each. The fewer files you have, the more likely you will only need to look in one file to find the paper you need. If you have to check more than one file to find the paper you need, you will learn to not trust your filing system, because the paper could be in any number of files. Keep it simple!

- All files should be divided into no more than five categories.

A category is a type of file. For example an insurance agent may have the categories of Customers, Sales & Marketing, Administration, Compliance, and Reference. Just make the categories broad enough so that everything can fit into that five. No sub-categories. Keep it

simple! Research has found that the human mind can remember up to five distinctions automatically without giving it any thought. Any more than five and we have to stop and think for a minute in order to keep it straight. The effort of having to stop and think each time you file is just enough effort to make you stop filing and start setting it aside in a pile. No more than five categories! You will probably struggle with this, trying to add just one more category; but don't do it. You simply need to come up with broader categories so everything can be contained in five categories or fewer.

Note: You do not want to have sub-categories or mini-categories within your three to five categories. That complicates the process and makes it more difficult for you to remember all the exceptions. Keep your system very basic – up to five categories with each paper alphabetized within each. No sub-categories. By keeping the filing system extremely simple, you will come to trust the filing system and will dare to file papers away, knowing you will be able to find them again.

The following is the step-by-step process you will use to divide your files into categories.

Make a list of every file heading you have created.

Example:

Board Meeting Minutes   City Bank
Catalyst Magazine   NAPO Newsletter

Look at the list and decide what your categories will be. They need to be chosen according to your way of thinking, so it is easy for you to use. Consider the different roles and responsibilities you have at work. Figure out how to group those roles and responsibilities into three to five categories.

Example:

Administrative	Financials
Sales & Marketing	Reference

After you have written down the three to five categories, appoint initials or some abbreviation for each category. For example Administration would be A or Ad, Financials would be F etc. Assign a different color for each category. You will use color coding on your hanging files and labels. It helps you make a clear distinction between the different categories. This speeds up the filing process.

Example:

Administrative	A	Blue
Sales & Marketing	SM	Red
Financials	F	Green
Reference	R	Yellow

Now go through your entire list and write the initial or abbreviation for which category each file belongs to.

Example:

A	Board Meeting Minutes
SM	Catalyst Magazine
F	City Bank
R	NAPO Newsletter

All files should be alphabetized within each category. This way, you only have to remember that it's in one of the five categories and it's alphabetized, to figure out where a paper you need may be located. Keep it simple! For example the insurance agent may need to retrieve an old print ad for a mailing. He has to decide which of the five categories that would belong in. In this case it is the Sales & Marketing category then he has to look it up alphabetically within the Sales & Marketing Category so he looks for his "Print Mailings" file.

• All papers inside a file folder should be placed with the top of the paper on the left side and the most recent paper added to the front of the file. That way, when you pull the file out and open it on your desk, the papers are right-side-up with the most recent paper on top.

When you are finished making your new, color-coded, finished files (See **Obtaining the Right Container for Paperwork**), transfer all documents out of the old, preliminary files into the new, finished files. Once all the documents are transferred, put the new files into the appropriate drawers. The categories that are accessed the most often should be stored at the most convenient locations. Of course, your tickler system files get the most convenient location of all.

Assigning homes for electronic files

Once every document and every folder has been sorted, look them over and see if there are any files that can be combined so there are fewer folders. Double check for accurate folder headings. When you have done that, create folders for the same five categories you made for the paper files. Click and drag every folder into the category's folder it belongs to. When you are done you should have five folders and within those five folders are a number of other folders in alphabetical order. Each of those folders is full of documents in an alphabetical order.

While you may utilize a different filing system for organizing your computer file (such as by file type or oldest to newest) it is my strong recommendation that you maintain your computer files in the same manner in which your paper files are kept (alphabetized by category). This way all your filing systems are consistent and you won't have to stop and think where things are located.

Assigning homes for things that belong in a drawer

Here is the step-by-step process for assigning a home to items that belong in a drawer other than a file drawer:

You want to organize drawers that are not file drawers so each item is always in the exact same place. This way, you can go on automatic pilot and find and return things without thinking about them and without looking for them.

a)   You should have emptied your drawers into the "Daily," "Weekly," "Monthly," and "Less Than Monthly" boxes when you did that stage of sorting.

b)   Line the bottom of the drawers with printer paper. Tape the papers together so you can pull the paper out in one piece and have the exact size and dimensions of each drawer.

c)   Measure how high the drawer is. This will tell you if you need the 1", 2" or 3 ½" drawer dividers. You can order the drawer dividers from www.ContainersThatFit.com. The height will also tell you which items will fit into the drawer, according to their heights. Label each paper with the following:

• The location of the drawer the paper was for (For example: Top Right Desk Drawer or Bottom Left Credenza Drawer)

• Which side of the paper represents the front of the drawer (For example: Front along the edge that is the front of the drawer.)

• The depth of the drawer.

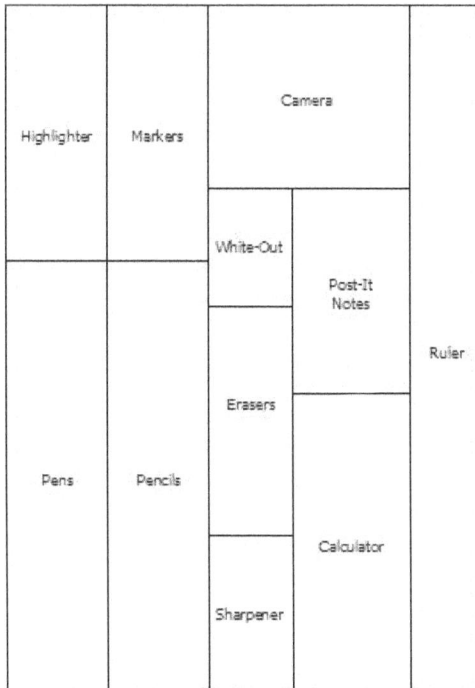

Draw a dotted line across the paper illustrating how far the drawer pulls out. You want to avoid building walls in a place that doesn't allow you to get to the things in the back because the drawer didn't pull out far enough.

d)   Go someplace where you can lay all the drawer papers out at the same time. Make sure the sides of the papers that represent the front of the drawers are facing you.

To assign permanent homes for things that belong in drawers, take your "Daily" box and place those items on your template (paper). Be sure to leave enough space for drawing lines (indicating where you'll be placing the dividers for each type of item). Leave ample space within the lines to set the item in the drawer and pull the item out without any difficulty. (Don't draw the lines yet.) You want to put daily items in the most convenient locations which is probably the front 2/3 of the desk drawers or the front 1/3 of other drawers. Be mindful of what regions each drawer is in. Place items in the drawers that are in or near the correct region. The telephone book should go in the drawer, closest to where the telephone belongs, that is deep enough. The printer ink cartridges should go in the drawer closest to where the printer belongs, etc.

After all the daily items have been assigned a place where they'll belong, take your "Weekly" box and place its contents on the (template) papers to assign the permanent home of those things for the drawers. These should be in a little less convenient location. Perhaps behind daily items or in drawers that are a little less convenient but still within arm's reach while you are in your desk area. Again, be mindful of what regions each drawer is in. Place items in the drawers that are in or near the correct region.

e)   Follow the same process with the "Monthly" box and the "Less than Monthly" box, each getting a little less convenient location. If you run out of drawer space, it is okay to keep "Less than Monthly" items somewhere outside of the immediate office space.

f)   Again, you want to remain mindful of how far the drawer pulls out and what part of the back of the drawer will be inaccessible if you have a tall drawer divider in front of it. Arrange the items in the back so the tall drawer divider is not blocking access to the space behind it when the drawer is fully extended.

g)   After you have all the items assigned and appropriately placed on the papers, look it over carefully and see if there are any changes you would like to make before you build the permanent walls.

h)   After you have approved your plan, take a ruler and draw walls around each item or group of items. After the walls are drawn, take one item at a time off the paper and write in its place what item belongs there. In other words, pick up the pair of scissors and write "scissors" in the place where the scissors were sitting. Put the item back in the appropriate box. Repeat this process with each item until the papers have been completely cleared off and properly labeled.

i)   You now have a home assigned to everything belonging inside a drawer. You now have the map you will use to install the drawer dividers.

Assigning Homes for Things that Don't Belong in a Drawer

After you have finished all three stages–sorting, installing the finished files and drawer dividers–you need to assign a home for everything that does not go inside a drawer and properly contain it.

Organize like items with like items. Put books together so they are divided into categories based on theme or subject. After all the books are in their appropriate place, label the shelves where the different subjects belong. (Clear labels with either white or black text may be used for a more aesthetic result.) Organize binders in the same fashion.

Organize CD's, keys, office supplies etc. by gathering all the CD's, keys, office supplies, etc. together to see how many you need to organize. Look through your office supply catalogs and pick which method of storage you prefer.

The fewer items you have on the surfaces the better you will be able to concentrate on the project you are working on. To boost your productivity you need to boost your ability to concentrate. Remember, to boost your ability to concentrate, you want to eliminate distractions. The number one cause of distraction is clutter.

11

Obtain the Right Container for Everything

The O in END CHAOS stands for Obtain the Right Container. This is the sixth step in the organizing process. This is the step when you purchase your containers and put everything into its container and label it.

Containers separate groupings and provide dividers, which help keep things organized. Be sure to you choose the right container, or you may just be adding one more thing to keep organized. Remember to make sure there is a proper fit between your things and the container and a proper fit between your container and the space you plan to keep it.

If the container is too small to contain all the items you are storing in it, it won't help you. If the container is too small or too big for the shelf, drawer, or space where it will be kept, it only adds to your disorganization. Measure the size of the contents and the size of the shelf where the container will be kept before you go to the store. If you purchase a container and take it to the office, only to find it's not quite the right size, you'll most likely just keep it and do the best you can with it. Returning it and still needing to find the right container is a pain and a hassle. In very little time, that container will become one more thing for you to move out of the way when you are looking for something.

Patrick turned his top desk drawer into his stash drawer. The drawer was three inches high and 18 inches deep. Patrick had tried to get his drawer organized before and had purchased a little drawer organizer that was a half-inch high, six inches wide, and 10 inches deep. It wasn't big enough to contain all the things he needed to keep in that drawer, so it was surrounded on all sides by the things that would not fit in the organizer. There was a two-and-a-half-inch space between the top of the organizer and the top of the drawer, ample space to stash and store papers and miscellaneous items he didn't want to deal with. Whenever he needed something out of the drawer, he would first open the drawer; then pull out the pile of papers and

miscellaneous 'stuff;' next, he would scoot the organizer and the things surrounding it out of his way, until he found the item he needed. Many times he couldn't find what he was looking for. His drawer organizer was not the right fit for the drawer. I got rid of the drawer organizer. I ordered one of those build-your-own organizer kits. It was three inches high and would contain everything he needed to keep in the drawer. It eliminated his ability to stash things, and it gave every item in the drawer its own assigned home.

The Right Container for Paperwork

To make your finished files, decide if you want to use Smead Viewable Labels or Avery Labels. Smead Viewable Labels provide better visibility than the Avery labels do. Thus it makes the filing experience a more pleasant experience and help you find paperwork quickly. However they are more expensive than the Avery Labels and they take a minute longer to create when you first make the files. First check to see if the Smead Viewable Labels (found in most office supply stores in the file supplies section) will fit inside the file drawer. There is a 50% chance they will stand up too tall and you will not be able to close the file drawer properly. To check, insert a blank Smead tab into five or six hanging files and put them inside the file drawer. Open and close the file drawer with the new files inside. See if the drawer opens and closes without difficulty. If the Smead Labels do not create a problem in closing the drawer, and if you have a color printer, you can use the Smead labels. If they do create congestion when you try to close the drawer, or if you do not have a color printer, use the Avery Labels.

Option A: Smead Viewable Labels

Smead Viewable Labels

When possible, I recommend files be made by using the colored hanging files, Smead Viewable Labels for both the tabs and the folders, and the 1st- or 3rd-position, manila file folders, depending on which side of the desk the files will be kept in.

Sit at your desk. As a rule, the Smead Viewable Tabs should be positioned closest to your body while you are sitting directly behind the desk. If the file drawer being used for the files is on the right-hand side, insert the Smead Viewable Tabs into the far left slot of the hanging files. This way, the tabs can be easily read whenever the drawer is pulled out. File folders can be purchased so that all the files are the same position. In other words so the label indexes are always in the same place. If the file label indexes are all on the far left side the box will say first position. If the file label indexes are all in the center the box will say second position. If the file label indexes are all on the far right side the box will say third position. Use the third position, manila file folders so that the file folder labels are on the right side of the drawer; this way the file folders are on the opposite side of the tabs.

If the file drawer being used for the files is on the left-hand side, insert the Smead Viewable Tabs into the far right slot of the hanging files. Use the first position manila file folders so that the file folder labels are on the left side of the drawer. The objective is to simply design the filing system so that the file folder labels are on the opposite side of the tabs.

Option B: Avery Labels

Avery Labels

If the Smead Viewable Labels do not fit inside your file drawer or if you prefer the Avery labels, use Avery Labels. Sit at your desk. The Pendaflex clear vinyl tabs should be positioned closest to your body while you're sitting directly behind the desk. If the file drawer being used for the files is on the right-hand side, insert the Pendaflex clear vinyl tabs into the far left slot of the hanging files. This means that the tabs will be closest to your body and thus easiest for quick reference. Use the third position manila file folders in order to keep the file folder labels on the right side of the drawer. This system keeps the file folder tabs on the opposite side of the hanging file tabs.

If the file drawer being used for the files is on the left-hand side, insert the Pendaflex clear vinyl tabs into the far right slot of the hanging files. Use the first position manila file folders so that the file folder labels will be on the left side of the drawer.

The purpose of the tabs and the folder labels is to provide easy identification of the files contents. Keeping the tabs and folder index labels on opposite sides of the drawer from each other keep them from interfering with each others visibility. That makes it easier to insert and retrieve documents. The tabs are more visible than the folder index labels. That is why you always put the tabs on the side of the drawer that is closest to your body. It improves the visibility of your files and makes the filing process easier.

The Right Container for Things that Belong in a Drawer

To install the drawer dividers you will need to have the following:

- Two sets of the appropriate height dividers for each drawer
- Extra clips that are the appropriate size for the dividers you are using
- Sturdy scissors
- The maps that you drew
- A label maker (can be found in any office supply store)
- Plenty of label tape in the ½ inch size
- Eight extra AA batteries for your label maker

Set up the files as follows:

1) Place the empty drawer in front of you with the map for that drawer on the right of it and all the supplies listed above on the left of it.

2) Lay the map inside the drawer and make a small pen mark on the walls of the drawer where the drawer divider walls you are building will make contact with the walls of the drawer. You are

going to pull the map out of the drawer; so you will need these pen marks to help guide you in putting the drawer divider walls back, in the right place.

3)   Take the map out of the drawer and lay it back in its place at the right side of the drawer.

4)   Refer to your map to determine how long you need the drawer dividers to be. Remember, the clips affect the length needed, so the dividers should be cut a little shorter (perhaps 1/8th inch shorter on both ends) than what the map calls for. Lay the divider down on the map and mark the divider at the length you want to cut it.

5)   Use your sturdy scissors to cut the drawer divider.

6)   It's very difficult to move a drawer divider clip, once you have stuck it onto the drawer or onto other drawer dividers. It's a little tricky to get them perfectly straight. To help make sure they are straight before you stick them on, slide the drawer divider into both clips without peeling off the tape on the clips and set them in the drawer in the appropriate place. Once you ascertain that it is in the appropriate place and the divider is lined up straight, make a tiny pen mark on the wall you are attaching them to, along the two sides of the clips. That way, after you have peeled off the tape on the clips and they are sticky, you have a clearly marked position of where to make it stick.

7)   Place the drawer divider clips on the drawer where you need them. Slide the drawer divider into the clips.

8)   Place the drawer divider walls that connect with other drawer divider walls by following the same pattern. Measure them on the map. Mark where to cut them. Cut them. Mark on the drawer dividers where you are going to place connecting drawer dividers. Be sure it matches your map. Place the clips at their appropriate locations. Slide the drawer divider into the clips.

9)   After all the drawer dividers are in their appropriate places you will want to label them clearly. Get out your label maker. Center the labels from left to right. For the sections in the front of the drawer, you will want to place the labels about 1/8th inch from the top of the drawer dividers. That way, when the items are in their places, they won't cover up the labels. However, when the drawer is in the desk you won't be able to see the labels in the back of the drawer if they

are up that high. You'll want to place the labels that belong in the back of the drawer so they are half way down the wall or divider. That way you can see the labels when the drawer is in the desk.

10) Test the placement of the labels by putting the contents inside the drawer where they belong and putting the drawer in the desk. Sit down in your chair and pull open the drawer. Can you see all the labels? Move them as needed, even if you have to make new labels.

11) Now all the drawer dividers should be in place and properly labeled. All the contents should be in the drawer, and the drawer should be in the desk or credenza where it belongs. Move on to the next drawer.

An organized drawer using drawer dividers.

Labeling

Label every container and every "home." When I first learned about the practice of labeling every home, I really resisted. I thought it would make my office look tacky. So I tried an experiment to find out for myself if it really made that much difference. I organized things like my files, drawers, shelves, etc. I used all the principles I had learned thus far, but I only labeled half of the homes. I worked with this for a while and documented my findings. I had to reorganize the items which didn't have their homes labeled twelve times more often than the items that had their homes labeled! So, I invested in a labeling machine, labeled the rest of the homes and have spent far less time maintaining my systems. Labeling your containers and the location where the containers belong will minimize your maintenance.

When you label the containers and label the spots where the containers belong, things get put back in the same place every time. It's like walking by a puzzle that is finished, except for one last piece. You are drawn to pick up that last piece and put it in the puzzle where it belongs. When members of your staff see labels and find that something is in the wrong place, they are drawn to fix it and put things where they belong. It won't happen every time, but it will happen often enough to make it worth the time spent labeling.

Also, it is easier to recruit help in keeping your organized systems organized if all items are clearly marked where they belong. You can assign your secretary to straighten a closet/shelf/drawer and he/she can leave it in the right condition, because everything is labeled.

For a free download of our special report "25 Quick Tips to Finally Get Control of Your Messy Environment" visit: www.OrganizeEnterprise.com/25quicktips.

12

Sustain Your System

The S The S in END CHAOS stands for Sustain Your Systems. This is the seventh and final step of the organizing process.

Daily Maintenance

Daily maintenance is required to sustain the areas you have organized. If you have already put the seven strategies in place, your daily maintenance should be minimal. You'll still need to look for things out of place and quickly put them back in place. The following strategies will ensure that there are very few things out of place.

1. Do all seven steps of the organizing process. Do them in the right order. Complete each step before moving on to the next step.

2. Maintain a proper fit between your things and the containers you are putting them in. Also, between your containers and the space in which you plan to keep it.

3. Store everything at the place where it is first used. Inside its region, within arm's reach.

4.   Organize so it is easier to put things away than it is to get them out.

5.   Eliminate extra steps and extra motions in the putting away process.

6.   Label, Label, Label.

7.   Maintain it daily.

Let me repeat that. Daily maintenance is required to sustain the areas you have organized. If you have already put the 7 strategies in place, your daily maintenance should be minimal. You'll still need to look for things out of place and quickly put them back in place.

It is important to commit to taking five minutes before you go to lunch and five minutes before you leave at the end of the day to straighten your office, no matter what. Five minutes before lunch and five minutes before the end of the day, stop what you are doing and straighten your office. File papers, tidy up drawers, clean off your desk and other surfaces. You don't have to work until the office is organized; you just need to work for five minutes each time and then stop. If someone is waiting for you to go to lunch, tell them you will be ready in five minutes then continue to straighten up your office. If you are in a hurry to get home at night, recognize that five minutes isn't going to make that big of a difference; so go ahead and straighten up your office. Developing the habit of taking five minutes before lunch and five minutes at the end of the day will keep your office organized and your systems intact. Maintaining it daily will keep your maintenance needs minimized.

Follow the work processing system with the tickler file the way I instructed you. That will help you stay organized and your space clutter free.

I encourage you to read this book once a year and to do what it says.

Semi-Annual Maintenance

You now know *how* to sort through everything, assign proper homes for things, contain and label them. Let me reassure you that life and business will require that you go through this process every six months to a year in order to maintain your space.

Part IV

Third Stage:
Target Awareness and
Activity Alignment

13

Goal Setting

The first thing you need to do to boost your productivity is to establish clearly defined business goals (targets). Get clear on what targets you are shooting for. The second thing is to organize your daily activity so it is in direct alignment with your chosen targets. Spend your time doing activities that draw you closer to your business goals. Delay tasks that interfere with those goals, such as tying up loose ends, responding to people's requests, or handling interruptions. Do those tasks after you have accomplished the ones that move you toward your goals.

For example establish the hours from eight until ten in the morning to be your protected time to produce work. Don't take phone calls or check your emails. Keep your office door shut with a do-not-disturb sign on it. Let your constituents know you will be available to help them from ten o'clock on but for the time between 8:00 a.m. and 10:00 a.m. you are not to be disturbed. Don't allow this time to be a catch up period for the myriad of loose ends dangling before you. Dedicate it solely to producing the work that impacts your success the most.

We establish goals in our minds and on paper, because it is the first step toward determining our life's destiny. Anthony Robbins puts it best in his Personal Power tapes when he says each one of your thoughts and actions is going to have an *effect* or *result* in your life.

Your results begin to "stack up" to take your life in a particular *direction*. For every direction there is an ultimate *destination* or *destiny*. What is important for you to decide is: "What is your ultimate destiny; what do you want your life to be?"

Consider your target(s)

What are you shooting for? What are your long term and short term goals? How clearly defined is your ultimate destiny? Since this is a book about boosting your productivity at work, we are talking about your career destiny. The more clearly defined your desired destiny is, the more likely and quickly you will arrive.

When I first started my organizing business I had a difficult time determining my businesses direction. I worked with a very talented business coach, Wendy MacDonald of Spectrum Solutionz. She had me work through a process of clarifying where I was in the moment and where I wanted to be at different stages of my career. It was an empowering and impressive exercise. I wrote on a card some goals I wanted to have accomplished by the end of the year. I couldn't conceive how I would reach those goals in such a short time. One year later Wendy mailed me that card and I was amazed to see I had reached and even surpassed all the goals I had written on the card. Clarifying your direction and chosen destiny makes it so much easier to hit your target.

I turned around and conducted the same exercise with Drake. Drake decided the target he was shooting for was to increase his business and profits by 20% each year and to be able to sell his company for 20 million dollars in 20 years. At his one year, three year, and five year deadlines he surpassed his goal of 20% annual increase. He is right on schedule for his retirement goals. I recommend that you go through the same exercise Drake and I did. Set your goals and establish the dates for when you want those goals met by.

Take time to clearly define your career targets (goals) by writing down your priorities. Be as specific as you can. Decide what you want your work to be about. Decide what you want it to stand for. Decide what the accomplishments and experiences are that you want to obtain before your career is over. Without putting limitations on yourself, consider what your ideal reality would be. Think through every detail. Clearly define it.

Organize Your Office for Success

EXERCISE

GOAL SETTING

First clarify where you are in the moment. Where do you stand in your career right now? What is your company/career like? What is your part in it?

_____

_____

_____

What are the five elements of success that are most important to you? In other words, what five elements do you want to structure your business/career around? I recognized that the five elements of success for me were profit, flexibility, growth, influence, and fun. Those were the elements in my career that needed to be thriving in order for me to feel that I was successful. Whenever I needed to make a business decision I looked at the five elements of success as a guide for my choices. What are your five elements of success?

1) _____

2) _____

3) _____

4) _____

5) _____

Now explain _why_ those five elements are important to you in developing your "Ultimate Business or Career."

_____

_____

_____

Organize Your Office for Success

What will your company/career look like after your ultimate business or career is established? What will be your part (role) in it? Be as specific and inclusive as you can be.

_____

_____

_____

How many hours a week do you work now? _____

How many weeks a year do you work now? _____

How large is your sphere of influence now? _____

How much money are you making now? _____

How many hours a week do you want to work
in your ideal career? _____

How many weeks a year do you want to work
in your ideal career? _____

How large of a sphere of influence do you
want to have in your ideal career? _____

How much money do you want to be making in
your ideal career? _____

Once you have your career's destiny defined, break it down into smaller increments. Clearly define your 20-year, 10-year, 5-year, 3-year and 1-year goals. Determine what you need as your 20-year goals in order for you to be on track for achieving your career's ideal destiny. Continue to break it down. What would you need to accomplish in the next 10 years in order to achieve your 20-year goals? Follow the same process to set 5-year, 3-year and 1-year goals. You could even take it so far as to plan six-month, three-month and one-month goals. After that, it is very easy to determine what you need to be doing this next week in order to achieve your ideal career destiny.

Organize Your Office for Success

EXERCISE

BREAK IT DOWN INTO SMALLER GOALS

What are your business/career goals 20 years from now?

_____

_____

_____

Time passes without you realizing it. In order for you to track your goals and your success you need to specify when the 20 year point arrives. What will the date be 20 years from now?

_____

What are your business/career goals ten years from now?

_____

_____

_____

What will the date be ten years from now? _____

What are your business/career goals five years from now?

_____

_____

_____

What will the date be five years from now? _____

What are your business/career goals three years from now?

_____

_____

_____

What will the date be three years from now? _____

What are your business/career goals one year from now? Be as detailed as you can be.

_____

_____

_____

What will the date be one year from now? _____

Align your activity to hit the target

Once you have established one year goals, it is easy to convert them into your daily activities by answering the following questions. These are the activities you need to be doing this week for you to hit your six month goals.

EXERCISE

GOALS CONVERTED INTO ACTIVITIES

What are your business/career goals six months from now?

_____

_____

_____

What activities do you need to do for the next six months to reach your six-month goals?

_____

_____

_____

Organize Your Office for Success

What are your business/career goals three months from now?

_____

_____

_____

What activities do you need to do for the next three months to reach your three-month goals?

_____

_____

_____

What are your business/career goals one month from now?

_____

_____

_____

What activities do you need to do this month to reach your one-month goals?

_____

_____

_____

Organize Your Office for Success

What are your business/career goals one week from now?

_____

_____

_____

What activities do you need to do this week to reach your one-week goal?

_____

_____

_____

14

Knowing How to Do It

Now there is a gap between deciding what you want to do and knowing how to do it. Let me share with you a story when I knew what I wanted to do but I didn't know how to go about it. I borrowed this story from my Organize Your Home in 10 Minutes a Day book. It makes a good point so I want to share it with you here.

I had a summer job at a fish hatchery following my senior year in high school. On my first day of the job, the rangers started me off by taking me to a hill where the grass was high enough to tickle your kneecaps, and told me to mow it. I didn't know a lot about mowing lawns but I knew I wanted to do a thorough job, so I set the mower on the lowest setting. It kept choking on me so I'd have to start it up again, but I was determined to do a thorough job so I kept doing it. It kept choking on me and I kept pushing it, all the while thinking, "This is not working!" Finally, it wouldn't start up again. It was dead. So I pulled it behind me to the ranger who repairs the equipment and I had to tell him, "I broke it".

He said, "O.K." and sent me down to another area and told me to weed it. I took the weed eater, and you know how when the line breaks you're supposed to give it a little tap and more line will come out? I was weed eating up against a chain link fence and it kept breaking the line. I kept tapping it and it kept breaking. Again I found myself thinking, "How am I supposed to do this?" I tapped it a little harder and it kept breaking. I kept tapping harder and harder, until finally it wouldn't play any more. I realized I broke the machine. I didn't want to have to tell the ranger I broke something else, so I just started weeding with my hands. I was just digging up those weeds. Again I had the thought, "This is not working!" Finally I got it done. I was tired and sweaty, but I was proud of myself for a job well done. I went back to the office and told them I had done a thorough job. There was not a weed left standing. They asked what happened to the weed eater and I had to confess, "I broke it, so I just weeded with my hands, but I did a thorough job."

One of the rangers asked, "You didn't pull up the trees did you?" I said, "No I didn't pull up any trees, there weren't any trees down there, but I sure did a good job on the weeds." The rangers looked at each other and they decided they had better go look for themselves. Sure enough, I had pulled up a dozen perfectly good young trees.

So they thought about what they should have me do next. They decided the safest thing was to have me use the riding lawn mower and mow the wide open places where there was no chance of me killing any trees. I got on the riding lawn mower. I was going along and I came to a place where there was a meter and some pipes coming out of the ground. I wanted to do a thorough job, so I drove forward and then put it in reverse, trying to get as close as I possibly could. I kept pulling forward, then backing up, each time getting a little closer. I'm not sure how, but I somehow got the front left wheel stuck between two pipes. Kind of like a car parallel parked with a car jammed up against the front of him and a car jammed up against the rear. I was really getting irritated now. I did not know how to get myself out of this mess!

I was not about to tell the rangers, I was going to fix this myself, so I worked it and I worked it. Have you ever seen those cartoons where a car runs out of gas? Its tires all of a sudden go "phhhhh" where the tires are now horizontal, instead of vertical. Somehow I strained this little driving lawnmower until its front two tires were horizontal instead of vertical. I screamed out loud, "Augh! I do not know how to do this!" I had no choice but to tell the rangers "I broke it." They said, "All right, no more yard work! Go sweep out the runways."

When the fish are taken from a runway, all that is left was the "guck" – dead fish, fish poop, old fish food, etc. – stuck to the bottom of the runway. So, wearing big hip wader boots, I walked along the top of a runway wall pushing a broom and cleaning the guck the best I could. I got to the end of the runway and there was this little strip of guck that I couldn't reach from the wall I was on. Since that was not working, I looked around for ideas. There was another wall about four or five feet away from me. I decided to lunge forward spread eagle style and grab that other wall with my hands, kick my feet over; so I'd be on that wall and could reach that little strip of guck. On my side of the wall I was lunging towards was a four foot drop into two feet of guck. On the other was a four-foot drop to a cement driveway. So, being the intelligent person that I was, I lunged toward that other wall. After I grabbed it with my hands, I kicked off of the first wall. I began to swing my feet over to the other side, but instead of swinging smoothly across, I somehow managed to get my hip wader boots tangled in an overhead cable. So, there I was standing on my hands, feet tangled, trying to get free, and recognizing I was in trouble. Well, I clearly did not know what I was doing!

I somehow managed to kick free. I went past the wall, down the four foot drop onto the cement driveway, and landed directly on my face. I jumped up to see if anyone was watching, and acted like nothing happened.

You know how your face throbs when it gets hit hard? Well, mine was doing that, but I didn't think anyone else would be able to tell. So, I went back to the office. I must have had blood and scratches all over the side of my face, because when I walked in a ranger said, "What happened to your face?" Before I could get a word out, another ranger in the room said, "She broke it!"

The funny part of that story is that not only did they keep me on for that entire summer but they wanted me to come back the next summer. They said they couldn't buy such good entertainment. I declined.

Once you get clear on your career goals you need to create a plan of how to go about reaching those goals. Part of creating a plan is to foresee problems you may run into and mapping out solutions of how to deal with those problems.

Overcoming Problems and Obstacles

When possible, you want to foresee problems and design an effective plan to overcome them. Otherwise we set goals and our plans are derailed by the problems that arise. It is important to foresee those problems and determine answers and solutions ahead of time so we are not derailed when the problems arise.

EXERCISE
FORESEEING PROBLEMS AND DESIGNING SOLUTIONS

Organize Your Office for Success

What are the problems you are facing in your business/career? What are the underlying causes? What is your plan to overcome the problems?

Problem #1:	Plan to overcome the problem:
Problem #2:	Plan to overcome the problem:
Problem #3:	Plan to overcome the problem:
Problem #4:	Plan to overcome the problem:
Problem #5:	Plan to overcome the problem:

Organize Your Office for Success

Most executives begin each day with a stack of "To Do" items—whether the "To Do's" are phone calls to make, emails to respond to, projects to work on, or deadlines to prepare for. Make sure your first priorities are the activities that will cause you to reach your six-month goals. Just make sure you don't set your priorities based on what is screaming the loudest. You may think that this isn't a reasonable suggestion, but it is. Prioritize based on what is most important, not what is most urgent.

Drake had a constant flow of employees at his door needing his attention, phone calls coming in needing his attention, etc. I trained him to ask himself a very important question as each thing came up. He asked himself, "Is what I'm working on more important than this interruption or is this interruption more important than what I'm working on." Being clear on his goals and on what activities led him to reach his goals he was able to make good decisions and take the right actions to create the success he was shooting for.

Processing the "screaming to do's" in the manner described earlier in the book will minimize the amount of urgent tasks and allow you to spend your time on the important tasks. Remember to discard, delegate, streamline, follow up, handle interruptions properly, gather, filter, prioritize and act on your work etc.

There will always be external forces causing things to become urgent. You can waste a career and a lifetime responding to what others dictate is urgent. If you want to reach your business goals, you have to make sure you line up your efforts/activities to hit the target. You have to make sure you are spending your time on what leads you to your goals, not just on "stuff that comes up."

15

See Your Targets Clearly in Both Your Conscious and Subconscious Mind

In my own quest to get organized I found the most difficult hurdle for me to overcome was my own belief system about what it means to be organized. I had to make changing my "internal environment" as much of a life study as changing my "external environment." I read a dozen books on the subject. Some of them I read six or seven times. I worked with three different coaches to help me be successful. I found adjusting what was going on inside my head provided a monumental leap forward on adjusting what was going on in my reality. I want to help you make the same leap. It is possible that the greatest obstacle to getting organized at the office and boosting your productivity will be the obstacles you have created in your own mind. In my experience as a professional organizer, I have found the psychological obstacles are the most difficult for people to overcome. It is necessary to address the psychological / mind issues in order to create lasting change.

Sarah attended one of my speeches. The speech motivated her to get organized at the office. She did some de-cluttering and made new files. However deep inside her nervous system Sarah associated keeping everything organized to being a pain and a bother. Something she really didn't want to bother with. She didn't really believe that it would benefit her that much. After a short time Sarah's resolve to keep things organized faded. She reverted back to her old way of doing things. She wasn't able to enjoy the benefits of improving her productivity at work. A typical day at work was stressful for Sarah. She continued to work a lot of overtime hours. She was never the one considered for promotions because she had a difficult time managing the responsibilities she already had.

Do you want to organize your office in a way that will last? I assume that is why you are reading this. Then, you have to first address what you think, believe, associate, and feel about getting organized at the office. I'll teach you how. Your behavior will *eventually* carry out whatever your thoughts and beliefs dictate.

The human nervous system *needs* to have all the elements that create change to be congruent with one another. The elements that create change are thoughts, beliefs, what you associate pain and pleasure to, feelings, and behaviors. You can try to make a change by changing one element, such as behavior. However, without changing the other four elements of thoughts, feelings, associations to pain and pleasure, and beliefs, your nervous system will eventually make you uncomfortable. It will cause your behavior to revert back so all five elements can be congruent with each other, working as one. If you try to get organized at the office by simply changing your behavior, you will fail in the long run.

Have you ever wanted to lose weight or get into better physical condition? You learned the right way to eat healthily and exercise. Did you find that even though you gained the knowledge of how to diet and exercise, you couldn't get yourself to actually do it on a consistent basis?

have you ever wanted to save your money for something, but something else came along that caused you to spend your money elsewhere. Perhaps you learned how to manage your money, but in the bumpy course of life you were not able to allocate it as perfectly as you knew you should.

I've heard it said, "I know how to organize. I just can't bring myself to do it." Do you want to get organized at the office? It's not enough to know how to do it. You have to find the secret that gets you to do what you know. That secret lies in understanding how the human brain and nervous system work. They share a common purpose. That purpose is to learn what will cause pain and what will cause pleasure. It is to do whatever it takes to help you to avoid pain and to gain pleasure.

Your brain and nervous system drive your behavior according to their interpretations of the reality you experience. Not based on the reality or the experience itself. There is a difference between your reality and your brains interpretation of that reality. Perhaps you have seen this demonstration before.

(Perception set from Myers Psychology, Eighth Edition)

Look at the center picture and describe what you see. Some people interpret this picture by seeing a man playing the saxophone. Other people interpret this picture by seeing the face of a woman. Look at the two interpretations of the center picture as found on the left and on the right.

The reality (which is the picture itself) did not change. Both interpretations of the reality were there the entire time. Now, look at the picture of the organizing experience you hold in your imagination. The reality may be that you significantly reduce the clutter and improve your productivity. One person may interpret that reality as a source of social, mental, or emotional discomfort or irritation, causing feelings of loss or sacrifice, frustration, or embarrassment, a source of creating conflict with co-workers or associates, or not wanting to commit to the time or energy spent on that activity.

Another person may interpret significantly reducing the clutter and improving their productivity as a source of freedom, hope, lightening their load, creating more time for them to do what they choose, making themselves and their office more comfortable physically, mentally, socially, emotionally, financially, and spiritually. They may see it as exercising their right to shape their own environment and quality of life to be the way they want it to be.

You may have the interpretation that getting your office organized requires you to lose time, money, and comfort. The challenge with that interpretation is that it establishes some limitations for your life. It requires you to stay stuck in a very limited, confined reality. It is important that you remember that your interpretation is merely an interpretation. Study the picture in your imagination. Take a moment to find the other interpretation.

All through life you have had experiences. Throughout each experience your brain and your nervous system interpreted whether it was painful or pleasurable. You developed a collection of those interpretations and your brain and nervous system came to conclusions about what certain things mean to you. All these experiences, interpretations, and conclusions are filed away in your brains and nervous systems database. We call those neuro-associations. Currently you look at getting organized at the office and your brain researches its database looking for some reference of what that will mean to you. What you associate to that. It picks up all the little experiences, interpretations, and conclusions you have filed away. According to what it finds, it will tell your nervous system that getting organized at the office will lead to pain or it will lead to pleasure. Your nervous system will create strong feelings throughout your system that make you either highly motivated or highly de-motivated or discouraged at the prospects of getting organized at the office.

Now, in truth, what most of you develop are mixed associations where you associate some pain and some pleasure to getting organized at the office. You also associate some pain and some pleasure to leaving things the way they were. It creates in you a tug-of-war where you want something, you work on it, you sabotage your efforts, and then you beat yourselves up for your sabotaging your efforts. You are not 100% motivated to get organized at the office because you link up pain to that result as well as pleasure.

You may wonder what pleasure you derive from staying disorganized at the office. When it comes to letting your disorganized day stay the way it is, you may associate pleasure in the form of escaping the effort required, comfort in hanging onto what is familiar to you, joy in the activities you get to do instead of organizing your office, or feelings of wealth due to the abundance of your possessions and activities.

Here is the bottom line. If you want to be motivated to get organized at the office, you need to explore what neuro-associations your brain and nervous system have linked up to that experience. Erase the associations you no longer want and establish better associations to get you where you want to be. It's kind of like getting on your knees and checking out your flower garden. You examine each plant to determine if it is a flower or a weed. If it is a weed, you pull it out. You plant a beautiful flower in its place. If it is a flower, you leave it there. You may even water and fertilize it to make it stronger. If you really want a beautiful flower garden, you plant more flowers. The more flowers you plant the more beautiful your flower garden will be.

In the same manner you need to search your mind to examine your neuro-associations garden. If you find you associate something negative to getting organized at the office, you pull it out. If you find you associate getting organized at the office to being painful, reject those beliefs/associations and plant new ones in their place. Replace it with a positive association or affirmation. If you really want to be highly motivated, you want to plant additional associations that support your desire to be organized at the office. Plant associations in your mind that if you don't get organized at the office, it is going to lead to pain. Plant associations that if you do get organized at the office, it is going to lead to pleasure.

What if you were to switch the associations you link up in your brain as to what you associate pain and pleasure to? What if you were to discover the costs or the pain of letting your disorganized day at the office stay the way it is? What if you were to link up so much pain to leaving it that way that you would do anything to avoid experiencing that pain? What if you were able to switch your associations of what equals pleasure? What if you saw an organized office as something so pleasurable you would do anything to attain it? Later in this chapter I'll teach you how to do that.

My favorite example of changing one's associations is the story of Scrooge in Charles Dickens' Christmas Carol. Scrooge had three "Motivators" visit him in the night and help him link up so much pain to staying the way he was that he totally changed his outlook and behavior in one night.

Why leave the associations you have linked up in your brain to whatever has been formed by a myriad of happenstance? Why not organize your associations so they empower you to behave in accordance to what you know would make your life better? This book will lead you in an exercise that will help you recognize what associations you have in your brain. It will teach you how to realign them in a way they makes sense to you. This book will help you link pain to not getting organized at the office and pleasure to getting organized at the office. That way your associations will highly motivate you to do what you know.

A couple of years later Sarah realized once again that she really needed to get better organized at the office. She called me for a consultation. We did the following exercise together. At first she tried to brush lightly over the questions and her responses. It wasn't that meaningful to her. I encouraged her to take the time to really consider the questions and to give specific answers that were meaningful to her. An amazing power was unleashed. She aligned her associations in such a way that impacted her for the rest of her life. She made permanent changes in how she did things. She boosted her productivity significantly. Over the next five years she received two large promotions and was able to maintain a schedule of leaving the office at 4:30 in the afternoon. She was happier, healthier and had stronger relationships with family and co-workers.

16

Organizing Your Neuro-Associations: Financial Pain

Find a quiet place where you will not be interrupted. Quiet your mind. You are going to write lists on paper, then record them on an audio cassette. Listening to your audio cassette daily will keep you motivated during the entire organizing process. You want to be sure to write all your responses down. Don't just think them in your head.

Today you are going to experience both pain and pleasure. The more intensely you can experience these states, the more good it will do you in changing your associations. Your nervous system has to feel the pain and pleasure at an intense enough level for it to link up new associations. Although you may feel great pain I assure you we will leave this exercise feeling great pleasure. It's important you don't leave this exercise half way through. You don't want to leave it while you are still feeling pain. Follow through to the end.

List the ways a disorganized office has cost you *financially.* It is going to require you to stretch your thinking to come up with all the ways, but it is important that you do. The more significant each one of the costs is the more it will motivate you. Don't cut corners here. Do your very best to come up with costs that are truly meaningful for you.

You want to make these as heavy and as tremendous of a cost as you can. How high of a price have you paid over the past 5–20 years? Spend some time thinking about it. Write it down. How high of a price will you end up paying over the next 5–20 years if you continue to work in a disorganized office? These costs should be so intense for you that

you can feel a physical weight bearing down on you from the heaviness of that price. Take time to feel the price you have paid and will continue to pay.

I hesitate to list possible costs for you. My experience has shown that if I say it, you will discount or dispute it. If you say it, it must be true. I would rather you thought of the costs on your own. However, there is value in my listing some possibilities for you to consider. I strongly encourage you to give careful consideration to the possibilities I have listed. Denial does not help you. It only keeps you stuck in the condition you have been in for some time. Break free! I believe in you. I know you can do it. Be honest and forthright about the ways the disorganization has cost you. Break free of chaos' bondage! You can do it. Some financial costs you may want to think about are:

1) All the clutter in your office, mind, and schedule was purchased one way or another. You paid for it either outright or indirectly. If you really want an eye opener, look at the contents of your office, mind, and schedule. Make a guesstimate of what those contents cost you. Take time to feel the pain before moving on. Feel it as intensely as you can.

EXERCISE:

WHAT HAVE THE CONTENTS OF YOUR OFFICE, MIND, AND SCHEDULE COST YOU?

_____

_____

_____

2) A highly disorganized office can be depressing. It is common for people to think "I have got to get out of the here." Tell me truthfully. Have you ever felt like you needed to get out of the office or you have got to get work off your mind? Did you run some errands which included some way to spend money. Spending money as a way to change your state of mind is a common practice. How much money have you spent over the past 20 years doing this? Be honest. Come up with a dollar figure. Take time to feel the pain before moving on. Feel it as intensely as you can.

EXERCISE:

WHAT HAS CHANGING YOUR MENTAL STATE COST YOU?

_____

_____

_____

3) What other forms of stress management have you paid for because the disorganized day at the office was depressing or stressful? Think of all the recreational outlets you have spent money on. Going out for a dinner and a movie. Paying a babysitter. Going on vacation. Renting a video, book, or game. Purchasing fast food because you didn't have time, energy, or desire to prepare your own meals. Purchasing convenience foods at the grocery store which are much more expensive than foods that take time to prepare. Spending time and money on hobbies and their supplies. Purchasing items to make the work experience more comfortable such as decorations, equipment, containers, etc.

Organize Your Office for Success

The list goes on and on. Think of these things one at a time and calculate how much you have spent over the past 5–20 years. Take time to feel the pain before moving on. Feel it as intensely as you can.

EXERCISE:

WHAT HAS FORMS OF STRESS MANAGEMENT COST YOU?

_____

_____

_____

4) A disorganized office creates stress. If it is disorganized for very long, it creates a chronic level of stress in your system. Chronic stress contributes to a vast number of physical and mental ailments. How much money have you spent in the past 20 years on medical bills that the ailment could have been related to stress? Include doctor's visits, prescriptions, and tests, lost work, physical therapy, massages, chiropractic, therapy, counseling, hospitalizations, anesthesia, dietician, and ibuprofen. Include it all. Come up with a dollar figure of what it has cost you over the past 5–20 years. What will it cost you in the next 5–20 years if you remain in the disorganized office?

EXERCISE:

WHAT MEDICAL EXPENSES HAS THE STRESS COST YOU?

_____

_____

_____

5) It is not enough that you paid for the clutter when you first acquired it. Now you are paying for it again by paying for the expenses of storing it and caring for it. Consider the amount you have paid in the past 5–20 years for your office rent, heating and air conditioning, lighting, and the cleaning of your office. You may think, "We would have paid that anyway so we could work in the office,"

but if your stuff is there you are not paying for it as working space you are paying for it as storage space. Storage space for all your clutter. Take time to feel the pain before moving on. Feel it as intensely as you can.

EXERCISE:

WHAT HAS THE OVERHEAD & MAINTENANCE OF IT COST YOU?

_____

_____

_____

6) Consider the lost income opportunities since your time, thoughts, and energy were consumed with managing the disorganization. If you had exchanged the time spent looking for things and distracted by the clutter for time spent generating income, how much could you have made over the past 5–20 years? Take time to feel the pain before moving on. Feel it as intensely as you can.

EXERCISE:

WHAT HAS IT COST YOU IN MISSED OPPORTUNITIES?

_____

_____

_____

7) Consider the money you have spent hiring services from other people or companies because you didn't have time to get around to it. Home or office improvements, repair, cleaning, maintenance, auto repair, cleaning (carpets cleaned, windows cleaned, housekeeping), maintenance, yard improvements, care, maintenance, laundry or dry cleaning, etc. etc. etc. What about services for the office? Temporary help, janitorial services, professional organizer, administrative assistants, etc. There are more services available than we can shake a stick at. How many have you hired because you didn't have extra resources to do it

yourself. The resources could be your time, energy, thought, effort, training, practice, or patience. If your resources are consumed with dealing with a disorganized office you have to pay someone else to provide the resources to do these other services. Take time to feel the pain before moving on. Feel it as intensely as you can.

EXERCISE:

WHAT HAS PAYING FOR PRODUCTS OR SERVICES COST YOU?

_____

_____

_____

8) Alexander lost $675,000 in one year due to missed deadlines, poor customer service, and inaccurate billings. What are you losing? Take time to feel the pain before moving on. Feel it as intensely as you can.

EXERCISE:

WHAT HAS POOR QUALITY OF WORK COST YOU?

_____

_____

_____

9) Stretch your thinking. Add to this list. Think of as many costs as you can. The more costs you think of the more motivated you will be to tackle this organizing project.

EXERCISE:

IN WHAT OTHER WAYS HAS IT COST YOU FINANCIALLY?

_____

_____

_____

17

Organizing Your Neuro-Associations: Mental Pain

L ist the ways a disorganized day at the office has cost you _mentally._ Go through the same process as you did with your financial costs. Feel the pain!

1) Consider your ability to concentrate. Distractions are the number one obstacle to being able to concentrate. Clutter is the number one source of distraction. It may be clutter in your office, clutter in your mind, or clutter in your schedule. Clutter-free offices allow the people working in them to laser their focus and to accomplish amazing things.

EXERCISE:

WHAT HAS YOUR INABILITY TO CONCENTRATE COST YOU?

_____

_____

_____

_____

2) Consider the costs to your memory. What are the important details in your work you are dedicating your memory cells to? Have your memory banks reached their full capacity remembering all the tasks & documents you have? Where you saw them last? Whether or not they are in working order? Times you needed the items and couldn't find them? Also, what you could do if you can't find the items? There is not any room left in your memory for other, more important aspects of work. What ways have you spent your resources trying to help you remember things. Calendars, planners, post it notes, asking for reminder phone calls, telling your co-workers, "Don't let me forget to…" Getting organized frees up so much memory space. It is unbelievable. Take time to feel the pain before moving on. Feel it as intensely as you can.

EXERCISE:

WHAT HAS YOUR INABILITY TO REMEMBER COST YOU?

_____

_____

_____

3) Consider the costs to your creativity. The creator of us all took chaos and created order. What masterpiece, whether it is writing, strategizing, coordinating, or whatever, is more amazing than the creative masterpiece of this earth? Take time to feel the pain before moving on. Feel it as intensely as you can.

EXERCISE:

WHAT HAS LACK OF CREATIVITY COST YOU?

_____

_____

_____

4) Stretch your thinking. Add to this list. Think of as many costs as you can. The more costs you think of the more motivated you will be to tackle this organizing project.

EXERCISE:

IN WHAT OTHER WAYS HAS IT COST YOU MENTALLY?

_____

_____

_____

For a free download of our special report "25 Quick Tips to Finally Get Control of Your Messy Environment" visit: www.OrganizeEnterprise.com/25quicktips.

18

Organizing Your Neuro-Associations: Social Pain

L ist ways a disorganized office has cost you *socially.* Go through the same process as you did with your financial costs. Feel the pain! Some social costs you may want to think about are.

1) Consider the costs in your relationship with your co-workers. What price have you paid by having your relationship with your staff be that of you nagging, reminding, and complaining about their messy work or how they don't contribute enough around the office. What kind of an example are you providing for your staff if you work in a disorganized office? What kind of patterns are they going to follow? Are you O.K, with that? Take time to feel the pain before moving on. Feel it as intensely as you can.

EXERCISE:

WHAT HAS IT COST YOU IN YOUR RELATIONSHIP WITH CO-WORKERS?

_____

_____

_____

2) Consider the costs in your relationship with your boss and customers. How happy are they with you if the business affairs are a mess, you are in a bad mood, the staff is unhappy and the commitments are ignored? How long will they put up with that before they start to look somewhere else to have their needs met? That is too high of a price to pay! Are you going to end up paying it? Take time to feel the pain before moving on. Feel it as intensely as you can.

EXERCISE:

WHAT HAS IT COST YOU IN YOUR RELATIONSHIP WITH YOUR BOSS OR CUSTOMERS?

_____

_____

_____

3) Consider the costs in your relationship with the people in your industry. What

kind of a reputation are you establishing? How long will that reputation haunt you? I know it's tempting to hide behind our chaos so we don't have to spend any more time with people than absolutely necessary. How empty (and non-profitable) is life if the only relationships you have are with yourself and your immediate staff? It might sound good for a while but in the end it is a lonely and poor existence. Take time to feel the pain before moving on. Feel it as intensely as you can.

EXERCISE:

WHAT HAS IT COST YOU IN YOUR RELATIONSHIP WITH PEOPLE IN YOUR INDUSTRY?

_____

_____

_____

4) Consider the costs in your relationship with yourself. Do you experience harmony within yourself if the environment and tasks you have stewardship of is in disarray? Isn't there some element of feeling like things are not as they should be or as you want them to be? Are you at discord with your inner self because of the condition of your day at the office? Do you ever get to feel complete harmony and peace? How much does your disorganized day at the office impact that? How high of a sacrifice in self respect, acceptance, peace, and happiness have you made? Are you really prepared to spend the rest of your life feeling that way about yourself? That is an awfully high price to pay. Take time to feel the pain before moving on. Feel it as intensely as you can.

EXERCISE:

WHAT HAS IT COST YOU IN YOUR RELATIONSHIP WITH YOURSELF?

_____

_____

_____

5) Stretch your thinking. Add to this list. Think of as many costs as you can. The more costs you think of the more motivated you will be to tackle this organizing project.

EXERCISE:

IN WHAT OTHER WAYS HAS IT COST YOU SOCIALLY?

_____

_____

_____

For a free download of our special report "25 Quick Tips to Finally Get Control of Your Messy Environment" visit: www.OrganizeEnterprise.com/25quicktips.

19

Organizing Your Neuro-Associations: Emotional Pain

L ist ways a disorganized office has cost you *emotionally.* Take the ways that you have been paying an emotional price all these years and let it register in your nervous system for a while. Feel the pain. Let your brain link up your painful emotions so it will do anything to avoid that pain. Your brain and your nervous system will associate so much pain to being disorganized at the office that it will drive you to organize.

1) Consider how life is so short. Do you really want to spend your life filled with the emotions of shame, embarrassment, humiliation, mortification, frustration, irritation, hopelessness, exhaustion, rejection, anger, despondency, overwhelm, fear, worry, hate, dread, despair, and so on and so forth? These are the feelings experienced by people who work in offices with a lot of clutter and chaos. Maybe you think yours isn't that bad. Or maybe those feelings are so constant and familiar you don't even realize you are experiencing

them. Take time to feel the pain before moving on. Feel it as intensely as you can.

EXERCISE:

WHAT HAS IT COST YOU IN YOUR EMOTIONAL STATES?

_____

2) Consider the reverse. In being disorganized at the office you often sacrifice the experience of feeling comfortable, having self-respect, gratification, reassurance, happiness, feeling content with life, having hope, love, peace, harmony, satisfaction, excitement, feeling capable, having faith, belief, trust, security, anticipation, intrigue, and so on and so forth. Feel the weight of sacrificing those emotions for the past 5–20 years. COMBINED! Are you really prepared to sacrifice those emotional states for the next 5–20 years? Claim those happy states. They are yours for the taking. Organize. Take time to feel the pain before moving on. Feel it as intensely as you can.

EXERCISE:

WHAT EMOTIONAL STATES HAVE YOU SACRIFICED?

_____

_____

_____

3) Stretch your thinking. Add to this list. Think of as many costs as you can. The more costs you think of the more motivated you will be to tackle this organizing project.

EXERCISE:

IN WHAT OTHER WAYS HAS IT COST YOU EMOTIONALLY?

_____

_____

_____

20

Organizing Your Neuro-Associations: Spiritual Pain

L ist ways a disorganized office has cost you *spirituallly*. Go through the same process as you did with your financial costs. Feel the burden of that weight. Feel the pain.

1) Consider the cost in your relationship with your creator. Is your creator proud of you for the condition in which you live? Do you feel close to your creator when you are filled with all the negative emotions I mentioned above? Consider the spiritual growth you have sacrificed because you have spent your time looking for things you need and working in chaos. Instead of spending your time studying, practicing, and perfecting spiritual aspects of your life. What are the immediate consequences of those sacrifices?

What are the long term consequences of those sacrifices? How many of your loved ones do those consequences impact? Are you willing to live with those consequences? What is the price in spiritual development you have been paying for the past 5–20 years?

Organize Your Office for Success

What are you committed to doing from here on out? Take time to feel the pain before moving on. Feel it as intensely as you can.

EXERCISE:

WHAT HAS IT COST IN YOUR RELATIONSHIP WITH YOUR CREATOR/HIGHER POWER?

_____

_____

_____

2) Consider your spirit. Is who you are as a spirit much more than you have been demonstrating here on earth? Have you been sacrificing the opportunity to once and for all make your life here on earth consistent with the quality of your spirit which is who you really are? Are you willing to continue making that sacrifice for the rest of your life? What will that mean for you? It's just my opinion, but I think that would be ultimate pain. To stay so distracted by our cluttered disorganized lives that we never manifest our full potential. It's time to shout from the rooftops, "I will not be denied! And so I must organize!" Take time to feel the pain before moving on. Feel it as intensely as you can.

EXERCISE:

WHAT HAS IT COST YOUR SPIRIT

_____

_____

_____

3) Stretch your thinking. Add to this list. Think of as many costs as you can. The more costs you think of the more motivated you will be to tackle this organizing project.

EXERCISE:

IN WHAT OTHER WAYS HAS IT COST YOU SPIRITUALLY?

_____

_____

_____

21

Organizing Your Neuro-Associations: Physical Pain

L ist ways a disorganized office has cost you *physically.* Go through the same process as you did with your financial costs. Feel the pain! Some physical costs you may want to consider are.

1) When I ask people how a being disorganized at the office affects them physically, the most common response I get is it makes them tired. Often it is not the work we have done that makes us feel tired it is the amount of work we recognize we still need to do. How much time have you spent feeling tired? What did that feeling of fatigue cost you in your productivity? Take time to feel the pain before moving on. Feel it as intensely as you can.

Organize Your Office for Success

EXERCISE:

WHAT HAS IT COST YOUR ENERGY LEVELS?

_____

_____

_____

2) Clutter affects the sanitation conditions of the office. Poor sanitation has a negative affect on your physical well being. How many germs have multiplied in your office because of the happy habitat made available with your stacks of clutter? How many of those germs have you touched, breathed, or spread over the past 5–20 years. How

much time have you spent feeling sick instead of healthy? Take time to really think about it. Take time to feel the pain before moving on. Feel it as intensely as you can.

EXERCISE:

WHAT HAS IT COST YOUR SANITATION LEVELS?

_____

_____

_____

3) I mentioned earlier how chronic disorganization creates chronic stress in your system. Chronic stress causes a great number of physical and emotional health problems. What are the health problems you have had over the past 5–20 years? How many of those could have possibly been stress related? Take time to feel the pain before moving on. Feel it as intensely as you can.

EXERCISE:

WHAT HAS IT COST YOUR PHYSICAL HEALTH?

_____

_____

4) Consider the costs you have paid in your physical fitness. You have wasted a lot of time looking for things you need or dealing with the disorganization. You could have spent that time on an exercise routine or on preparing food that would keep you fit. If you had, how would your physique look today? How many pounds of fat have you been carrying around day after day because of that sacrifice you have made? How much energy have you missed out on because of the proportion of your body mass that is simply fat? What could you have enjoyed with those energy reserves? Take time to feel the pain before moving on. Feel it as intensely as you can.

EXERCISE:

WHAT HAS IT COST YOUR PHYSICAL FITNESS?

_____

_____

_____

5) Consider the costs in your physical grooming. What if you spent the time, money, and energy on developing a fantastic wardrobe, doing your nails, hair, teeth, skin, etc? What costs have you paid because you didn't look as nice as you could have? How much time have you spent not feeling good about yourself because of the way you look? Take time to feel the pain before moving on. Feel it as intensely as you can.

EXERCISE:

WHAT HAS IT COST YOUR PERSONAL GROOMING?

_____

_____

_____

6) Stretch your thinking. Add to this list. Think of as many costs as you can. The more costs you think of the more motivated you will be to tackle this organizing project.

EXERCISE:

IN WHAT OTHER WAYS HAS IT COST YOU PHYSICALLY?

_____

_____

_____

22

Organizing Your Neuro-Associations: Mixed Associations

Now it's time to address your mixed associations. On a separate page, list 20 negative things you associate with a highly organized office. It can be what you think about people who run a highly organized office. What you think it means if you always have a clutter free office. What it is going to take to maintain an organized office. It can be why you don't want to worry about keeping an organized office. List twenty negative things.

A painful association people make about being highly organized at the office is the concern that being organized to that extent is too strict or too structured. In other words, you *fear the loss* of freedom, flexibility, and control over your own life. Do you remember my definition of being organized at the office that you found at the beginning of the book? To be organized at the office means to have a structured schedule where activities are compressed and organized in a manner that enables you to perform at the height of efficiency and effectiveness. It means you have structured behaviors such as habits and routines that help you be efficient and effective in your work.

The Freedom of a Structured Schedule

A structured schedule and structured behavior gives you *more* freedom. It gives you "time freedom." Remember how you visualized you compressing the Legos together and stacking them carefully in place so they took less space in your container? When you add structure to your schedule meaning you compress each task and activity so it takes less time and you stack your tasks and activities in a structured manner throughout your day they take less time in your day (less space in your container). I have worked with dozens of clients on structuring their schedule and behavior. On average they have found this practice frees up two hours a day.

Phillipe reserved the time from eight until eleven in the morning for meetings. He compressed each meeting so they were scheduled to be 45 minutes long instead of one hour long. He put the meetings back to back so there was no time wasted in between meetings. He also structured all his outgoing telephone calls. He made all his calls back to back in one sitting. He was careful to get straight to business and keep the matters discussed as brief as possible. He didn't waste any time between calls and he kept the length of each call to a minimum. He did the same thing with his email. He checked it only twice a day and returned all emails back to back and kept his responses as brief as he could. He followed this pattern with all the activities and tasks that filled his day and he found that by doing this he was able to free up an additional two hours each day.

Patricia dealt with a high level of interruptions. If the interruptions took less than 60 seconds for her to deal with it she went ahead and took care of it. If the interruptions were going to take longer than 60 seconds she scheduled the interruptions into her day. In other words she would say "I'm in the middle of something right now, can I help you with that at (time of day) later today? She reserved a set amount of time each day specifically for dealing with lengthy interruptions. She scheduled them back to back and always for a little less time than what she thought she would need for them. That way she approached each issue in an efficient manner. By scheduling interruptions she was able to protect other times of the day for her work. She estimated this process saved her anywhere from an hour and a half to three hours a day.

Solomon reserved the first hour of each morning to meet with his administrative assistant. His administrative assistant would screen all his calls and emails throughout the day and would bring them to Solomon's attention during their morning meeting in order of their priority. Solomon would dictate assignments to the administrative assistant to handle all the emails and phone messages. Solomon's administrative assistant oversaw all scheduling for Solomon and would let him know what his schedule was for the day as well as have all documents in order for the scheduled appointments. If there were any preparations needed for the day's appointments Solomon would delegate as much as possible to the administrative assistant. The morning meeting would facilitate an exchange of mail, email, phone messages, schedule, assignments, accountability and follow up for all previous assignments. Solomon also had five heads of departments that needed his attention on a regular basis. Rather then interrupt each other all day each head of department had a set time to meet with Solomon each morning and go over any business, needs, ideas, and priorities. If a matter arose during the day and it could possibly wait until the next day's meeting it was held until the scheduled meeting. Solomon scheduled these meetings back to back immediately following his meeting with his administrative assistant. Solomon found that this process freed up two hours a day.

If a structured schedule and structured behavior frees up two hours a day, 365 days a year, 10 years a decade, eight decades a lifetime. That equates to 58,400 hours or 2,433 days that you get to use pursuing anything you choose. What would you do with that time? Would you pursue your life's passion? Would you exchange it for wealth, relationships, spirituality, or personal or professional development? You are free to choose what you do with that time. Your structured schedule and behavior gives you that freedom of choice. It gives you freedom from the limitations you experience in your current life. Limitations of wealth, rank or position. It allows you to have stress-free moments, comfort on the job, creativity, personal and professional development, quality time you get to spend with your spouse and children, and so much more.

Organize Your Office for Success

A structured schedule and structured behavior gives you freedom from stress. You are better prepared for every occasion. You don't have to consume your reserve of physical, mental, and spiritual energy adapting or responding to every little thing that comes up. Some people get addicted to the stress that a chaotic schedule or chaotic behavior creates. It gives them an adrenaline rush to be that stressed. Remember that having that stress consumes your reserves. It reduces what you are capable of handling. By getting rid of the stress that an unstructured schedule and unstructured behavior creates you increase your capabilities. The greater your capabilities are the greater your opportunities are. Another thing to consider is your quality of life. If you are stressed at work how does that impact your health, your relationships both at work and at home, your mental and emotional wellbeing, your passion for life?

Jared worked long hours. Every hour was highly stressful. He ran from one thing to the next and was constantly having to adapt to whatever crisis or interruption would arise. He was exhausted and felt out of control. We put some control back into his life and lowered his stress level by adding structure to his schedule and activity. Everything was assigned a home of where it belonged whether it was physical objects, appointments, mini-deadlines, or interruptions. It helped him feel like he was in control and like he could handle whatever crisis or interruption came his way.

A structured schedule and structured behavior gives you more flexibility. It opens doors of opportunity to you that were otherwise closed. It allows you to choose your path rather than to follow whatever path was laid out before you.

Drake followed routines throughout his day. One of the routines he followed at the end of the day was to spend five minutes tidying up his office and then prioritize his work for the following day. By doing this simple routine Drake kept the flexibility of choosing what work he did the following day. Working on what was truly most important to him rather than just reacting to whatever happened to scream for his attention. Drake also realized that by following the structured schedule and routines that Phillipe, Patricia, and Solomon did as mentioned above he too was able to save two hours a day. Every day Drake had total flexibility on what he did with those two hours. Some days he worked on a project that would advance his career.

Other days he went home early and spent some quality time with his wife. Other days he took someone in his business circle to lunch in order to strengthen the relationships that would help him reach his goals. It was totally up to him what he did with those two extra hours. Drake loved the flexibility this provided for him.

A structured schedule and structured behavior gives you more control over your own life. You are in control of how much time you spend in a meeting or on a telephone call. You control what time you start and end your work day. You control interruptions, work flow, the level of accomplishment, income, priorities... The list goes on and on.

You have a simple choice to make. Do you want to remain stuck and confined within the limitations of your old interpretation of what a structured schedule and behavior means to you? *Or,* Do you want to gain all the freedom, flexibility, and control over your own life that an empowering interpretation provides you? Which interpretation of a highly structured schedule and behavior are you determined to hang onto?

But I don't want to offend anyone...

Another painful association people make about being highly organized at the office is the concern that if they handle things too efficiently, it might offend others.

Success in business is largely due to success in relationships; so your concern about not offending others is a valid and legitimate concern. Many of my clients have shared the same concern. However, they found that they could increase how *effective* they were in their human interactions. Thus, they could get away with being *extremely efficient* as well, without offending anyone. Think about it. People don't care how much time you spend in a meeting or a telephone conversation. People don't come to like you and respect you because you spend more time hanging out at the water cooler shooting the breeze. What they care about is whether or not you care about them personally or whether or not you care about the projects you have in common.

There are several alternative ways to communicate to people that they are important to you, other than spending more time with them. Things such as: Giving a genuine smile both with your mouth and with your eyes when you first see them. Call them by name. Shake their hand by embracing their hand with both your hands. Tell them you appreciate them and their efforts. Tell them at the beginning of your conversation that you only have so much time. Tell them it's important to you that all their needs are addressed, so you want to get right to it. Praise them. Benefit their lives.

There are several alternative ways to communicate that the project is important to you other than spending more time in long winded meetings or conversations. Things such as: correctly *identify* elements of the project. Have all your responsibilities pertaining to the project appropriately handled. Give the project 100% of your attention during the time you *are* spending on it. Give timely communications to other people who are working on the project. Express appreciation for the project. Make a beneficial contribution to the project.

Remember that you set an example to the other members of your staff whether you mean to or not. How efficiently you handle matters will impact how efficiently they will handle matters.

But I might need that...

Another painful association people make about being highly organized at the office is the concern that if they throw stuff away, it will be like losing a piece of history, documentation, or a relationship that they might need again someday.

It is fascinating to me how the human mind links some things together that don't necessarily have anything to do with each other. (I do it too. Sometimes it takes hitting a brick over my head to get it through to me that there is no basis for that *link* or connection.)

My father was a religious man and he was a poor man. I don't remember exactly what was said but some how I grew up with the belief that if you are financially wealthy it means you don't have your priorities in the right place and your spirituality isn't a high enough priority. Now I know that is a false belief and one doesn't have anything to do with the other but that doesn't change the fact that I've got that belief linked up in my head. For a long time as an adult I found that if we got too financially comfortable I became very uncomfortable. I know some of my brothers and sisters face the same struggle. I had to realign my neuro-associations so I didn't associate so much pain to having financial security.

Rhett kept every paper from every project he ever participated in. For some reason he got it linked up in his head that he was erasing history if he didn't have all the paperwork involved during its creation. Soon his office became so full of paperwork from past projects that he was no longer able to function effectively on current projects let alone future projects. There were filing cabinets lining every wall. There were boxes of paper stacked on top of the filing cabinets. There were loose files all over his desk, stacked on the chairs and the floor. Rhett was buried in clutter. Yes, it is true that it is wise to keep documentation on past projects but not every single piece of paper used in the process.

Some people make the association that if they throw an item away and *just might* need it again some day, the most extreme and dire consequences will follow. Most things can be created again through another source. The time spent to recreate something won't even come close to the amount of time you waste buried in that clutter (as in the scenario with Rhett). There are very few things that truly create a life or death consequence should you get rid of your copy of it.

Do you want to know what to keep and what to get rid of? Check with your attorney, accountant, and manager to find out what paperwork and objects you really need to keep. That way you know you are keeping the documents you truly need, but you are able to get rid of all the documents you're merely feeling fearful about getting rid of . If you are the manager and there is no one higher up the ladder of leadership than you, ask yourself a simple question. *Under what circumstances am I really going to need this document again?* Only keep it if you can think of a specific circumstance when you WILL need it again, not when you MIGHT need it again. Chances are you can get it somewhere else if you ever need it again.

Of course you always have the option of scanning all the documents and keeping the information electronically. Just be careful to organize your electronic files so your computer database is not buried with cluttered documents.

Being organized just takes too much time...

Another painful association people make about being highly organized at the office is the concern being that organized takes too much time. This is another example of your *interpretation* of reality. I have elaborated extensively on how much time you *save* when you *take* the time to organize all along the way. Believing that organizing all along the way takes too much time is like believing that exercising takes too much energy. The truth of the matter is that exercising does not consume energy–it creates energy! Organizing does not consume time–it creates time! Remember the Legos exercise? Only by organizing everything that flows into your day can you fit everything within the eight hour time period. Only by taking the time to organize all along the way can you double your production capacity.

When you think of the phrase, "Highly organized at the office" what comes into your mind? Write down every thing that floats into your mind both good and bad. Don't scrutinize, reject, or exclude any thought. Take time to be as inclusive and thorough as you can. Then pin point which of your thoughts were a negative association to the phrase and list them below.

EXERCISE:

WHAT ARE THE NEGATIVE ASSOCIATIONS YOU HAVE WITH A HIGHLY ORGANIZED OFFICE?

_____

_____

_____

_____

_____

_____

_____

_____

_____

Now write a rejection statement for each of the negative things you associated with a highly organized office. These are statements that reject the old association. They may start out with, "It is not true that..." or "I no longer believe that..." Replace your negative associations to an organized office with positive affirmations that support an organized office mindset. Statements that begin with "I now know that..." "I now believe..."

EXERCISE:

WHAT ARE THE REJECTION STATEMENTS FOR THE NEGATIVE ASSOCIATIONS YOU HAVE TO A HIGHLY ORGANIZED OFFICE?

_____

_____

_____

_____

_____

_____

_____

_____

_____

_____

For a free download of our special report "25 Quick Tips to Finally Get Control of Your Messy Environment" visit: www.OrganizeEnterprise.com/25quicktips.

23

Organizing Your Neuro-Associations: Financial Pleasure

G et up and shake it off. Get out of your chair and stretch, bend, twist. Think happy thoughts. Plant 10 happy thoughts into your mind in order to interrupt the pattern of those painful thoughts. No less than 10. Do jumping jacks. Sing a happy song. Do what ever it takes to shake off the negative feelings or state you were in from doing this exercise. Then immediately do the following steps.

List ways an organized office will reward you *financially.* Make these rewards as grand as possible; the bigger the better. Again, it may be a stretch for you to come up with several ways but you can do it. You must do it. You need to recognize a substantial enough reward to compel your behavior to get the job done. What are the possibilities? How great of rewards will you experience over the next 5–20 years combined. Take time to feel the feelings of excitement, joy, anticipation, and satisfaction upon receiving those financial rewards. These ways should be so intense for you that you can't stay seated in your chair because you are so excited. Get into those feelings. Take time to let the feelings of exhilaration register in your nervous system for a while. Let it help your brain link up massive amounts of pleasure to maintaining an organized office. Really get into those feelings.

1) How much money will you save if you quit spending money to manage your state of mind? Look at the total amount you listed as financial costs. Multiply it by two. What would you like to do with that money? Invest? Care for the homeless? Remodel your home or office or build a new beautiful home or office? Travel? Get a nose job? What?

Imagine your checking or savings account with that much money sitting in it waiting for you to decide what you want to do with it. Take a few minutes to daydream of what you would do with all that money. Feel the excitement, intrigue, anticipation, hope, satisfaction, joy and all the other positive states of mind you get from having that kind of money in savings. Take time to feel the pleasure of those states before moving on. Feel it as intensely as you can.

EXERCISE:

HOW MUCH MONEY WOULD YOU SAVE AND WHAT WOULD YOU DO WITH THAT MONEY?

_____

_____

_____

2) Consider how much more square footage you would have in your office if you didn't have any of that clutter. Would it double the amount of space you have available to set up regions (activity centers or work stations) in your office that support you in what is most important to you? Would it triple it? What regions would you set up? How much profit, pleasure, reward, joy etc. would you experience from having those regions set up in your office? Take a few minutes to daydream about what activities you would set up in your office if you had the space. Imagine the pleasure you and your staff would experience participating in those activities. Take time to

feel the pleasure of those states before moving on. Feel it as intensely as you can.

EXERCISE:

HOW MUCH SQUARE FOOTAGE WOULD YOU FREE UP AND WHAT REGIONS WOULD YOU SET UP IN THAT SPACE?

_____

_____

_____

3) Consider the income generating activity you would do if you had an extra two hours a day to do it. Time you have saved not having to look for things or dealing with disorganization. If you could earn that income doing something you feel passionate about or something you love doing, what would you do to earn that income? You don't have to figure out the details. Just figure out your passions and imagine spending that time doing it. Imagine you have found some way to create a fantastic income with that time. What would you do with that income? Would you put in a swimming pool? Furnish your home from top to bottom? Finance a new hobby? Further your child's education? Get completely out of debt? Double your income by investing wisely? What can you really get excited about? Take time to feel the pleasure of those states before moving on. Feel it as intensely as you can.

EXERCISE:

WHAT INCOME GENERATING ACTIVITY WOULD YOU DO WITH THE TIME SAVED AND HOW WOULD YOU SPEND THAT EXTRA INCOME?

_____

_____

_____

4) Stretch your thinking. Add to this list. Think of as many rewards as you can. The more rewards you think of the more motivated you will be to tackle this organizing project.

EXERCISE:

IN WHAT OTHER WAYS WILL IT REWARD YOU FINANCIALLY?

_____

_____

_____

_____

_____

_____

_____

_____

**For a free download of our special report
"25 Quick Tips to Finally Get Control of
Your Messy Environment" visit:
www.OrganizeEnterprise.com/25quicktips.**

24

Organizing Your Neuro-Associations: Mental Pleasure

L ist ways an organized office will reward you *mentally*. Go through the same process as you did with your financial rewards. Feel the exhilarating lift in your spirits as you think about those mental rewards.

1) Consider the possibility of boosting your ability to concentrate by 75%. What mental tasks could you accomplish with that kind of concentration? You could quickly and easily get through the tasks of daily living. Then what? Would you further your professional development? Discover the cure for companies biggest problems? Solve dilemmas in such little time you didn't even realize you were facing a dilemma? Would you design something? What would it be? Would you increase your knowledge on something that interests

you? Or would you pursue the wisdom of the ages? Perhaps you would simply enjoy the freedom that comes from having things handled. Being completely free of worry or effort. Take time to feel the pleasure of the states you would experience doing those things before moving on. Feel it as intensely as you can.

EXERCISE:

WHAT MENTAL TASKS COULD YOU ACCOMPLISH WITH YOUR IMPROVED ABILITY TO CONCENTRATE?

_____

_____

2) Consider what you would retain in your memory if your memory cells were not committed to dealing with mental clutter. Would you memorize important writings? Would you strengthen your relationships by remembering special occasions, important events, or sensitive issues? What could you learn tomorrow because you still remember everything you learned yesterday? What would you gain from that? How would it benefit you? Would you like to be praised for having the memory of a steel trap where nothing escapes it? How much fun could you have with that? Take time to feel the pleasure of the states you would experience doing those things before moving on. Feel it as intensely as you can.

EXERCISE:

WHAT WOULD YOU BE ABLE TO RETAIN IN YOUR MEMORY AND WHAT WILL THAT DO FOR YOU?

_____

_____

_____

3) Stretch your thinking. Add to this list. Think of as many rewards as you can. The more rewards you think of the more motivated you will be to tackle this organizing project.

EXERCISE:

IN WHAT OTHER WAYS WILL IT REWARD YOU MENTALLY?

_____

_____

_____

_____

_____

_____

25

Organizing Your Neuro-Associations: Social Pleasure

List ways an organized office will reward you *socially*. Go through the same process as you did with your financial rewards. Feel the exhilarating lift in your spirits as you think about those social rewards.

1) Consider the benefits that would come from you having a better relationship with each of your co-workers. Would you be able to influence their work for the better? Perhaps help them avoid crisis? Perhaps you could inspire them to accomplish great things, experience great things and maintain quality relationships with others. Would you laugh with them? Feel more feelings of appreciation? Share an interest? If you could choose any kind of relationship to have with your co-workers what would it be? Does it seem unreal? It doesn't have to. Take time to feel the pleasure of those states you would experience before moving on. Feel it as intensely as you can.

EXERCISE:

WHAT BENEFITS WOULD COME FROM HAVING A BETTER RELATIONSHIP WITH YOUR CO-WORKERS?

_____

_____

_____

2) Consider the quality of relationship you would have with your boss or customers. Would the two of you associate feelings of happiness, enjoyment, appreciation, intrigue, if you weren't buried by the chaos of work? Can you imagine both of you being so excited about your projects. Would you be full of excitement for the opportunity to share your day with each other if you weren't worried about deadlines, responsibilities, finances, things that taxed you mentally or socially? If being free of disorganization freed you both up financially, mentally, socially, emotionally, spiritually and physically what profitable, fun, exciting, amazing thing would you approach together? How would that improve your bottom line? Take time to feel the pleasure of those states you would experience before moving on. Feel it as intensely as you can.

EXERCISE:

WHAT BENEFITS WOULD COME FROM HAVING A BETTER RELATIONSHIP WITH YOUR BOSS OR CUSTOMERS?

_____

_____

_____

3) Consider the quality of relationships you will develop outside of your immediate company. What doors of opportunity will those relationships open for you? Think. Think hard.

EXERCISE:

WHAT BENEFITS WOULD COME FROM HAVING A BETTER RELATIONSHIP WITH PEOPLE IN YOUR INDUSTRY?

_____

_____

_____

4) Stretch your thinking. Add to this list. Think of as many rewards as you can. The more rewards you think of the more motivated you will be to tackle this organizing project.

EXERCISE:

IN WHAT OTHER WAYS WILL IT REWARD YOU SOCIALLY?

_____

_____

_____

_____

_____

_____

**For a free download of our special report
"25 Quick Tips to Finally Get Control of
Your Messy Environment" visit:
www.OrganizeEnterprise.com/25quicktips.**

26

Organizing Your Neuro-Associations: Emotional Pleasure

L ist ways an organized office will reward you _emotionally_. Go through the same process as you did with your financial rewards. Feel the exhilarating lift in your spirits as you think about those emotional rewards. Consider the wide range of emotions you will experience when you are truly free of the chaos and clutter. Let those feelings fill your soul. Feel the joy. Feel the relief. Feel the hope. Really let your nervous system feel it

1) In having an organized office you often enjoy feeling comfortable, having self-respect, gratification, reassurance, happiness, feeling content with life, having hope, love, peace, harmony, satisfaction, excitement, feeling capable, having faith, belief, trust, security, anticipation, intrigue, and so on and so forth. How much better will your decisions be if you are in these states when you make them? How much grander will your accomplishments be if you are always in these positive states. How much happier will you be? Really think

about what it would be like to go through your life in the states I have mentioned.

EXERCISE:

WHAT EMOTIONAL STATES WOULD YOU ENJOY THAT ARE TRULY MEANINGFUL TO YOU?

_____

_____

2) Stretch your thinking. Add to this list. Think of as many rewards as you can. The more rewards you think of the more motivated you will be to tackle this organizing project.

EXERCISE:

IN WHAT OTHER WAYS WILL IT REWARD YOU EMOTIONALLY?

_____

_____

_____

_____

_____

_____

27

Organizing Your Neuro-Associations: Spiritual Pleasure

L ist ways an organized office will reward you *spiritually.* Go through the same process as you did with your financial rewards. Feel the exhilarating lift in your spirits as you think about those spiritual rewards. What will those spiritual rewards mean for you?

1) Consider your potential if you truly lived up to your spiritual identity.

EXERCISE:

WHAT IS YOUR POTENTIAL IF YOU TRULY LIVED UP TO YOUR SPIRITUAL IDENTITY?

_____

_____

_____

_____

169

2) Consider your strength, increased capacity, ability, happiness, and purpose.

EXERCISE:

WHAT IS YOUR STRENGTH, INCREASED CAPACITY, ABILITY, HAPPINESS AND PURPOSE?

_____

_____

_____

3) Stretch your thinking. Add to this list. Think of as many rewards as you can. The more rewards you think of the more motivated you will be to tackle this organizing project.

EXERCISE:

IN WHAT OTHER WAYS WILL IT REWARD YOU SPIRITUALLY?

_____

_____

_____

_____

_____

_____

28

Organizing Your Neuro-Associations: Physical Pleasure

List ways an organized office will reward you *physically.* Go through the same process as you did with your financial rewards. Feel the exhilarating lift in your spirits as you think about those physical rewards. Some physical rewards you may want to consider are:

1) What would your physique look like if you had ample time to take care of it? Would you be fit? Would you be strong? Would you be full of energy? Would you turn heads as you walked by? Consider the possibilities. Imagine the physique of your dreams and feel assured that you will have the resources to create that now that you are no longer wasting time at the office.

EXERCISE:

WHAT WOULD YOUR PHYSIQUE LOOK LIKE IF YOU HAD
AMPLE TIME TO TAKE CARE OF IT? WHAT WOULD IT BE
LIKE TO HAVE A PHYSIQUE LIKE THAT?

_____

_____

_____

2) Consider what your health would be like. You would be living in a
cleaner environment. Your new zest for life would improve the
quality of your health. You would have more time to eat right.
Imagine having a source of energy and stamina coming from your
core that helped you to achieve your wildest dreams. What would it
be like to FEEL healthy all the time?

EXERCISE:

WHAT WOULD YOUR HEALTH BE LIKE IF YOU HAD AMPLE
TIME TO TAKE CARE OF IT? WHAT WOULD IT BE LIKE TO
HAVE HEALTH LIKE THAT?

_____

_____

_____

3) Consider your personal grooming. Would you be well dressed?
Would your teeth be straight and white if you had the funds to
dedicate to that? Would your hair be groomed just the way you
would like it to be because you could focus on acquiring that now?
Would your nails be manicured and toes have a pedicure? Would
your skin be clear because you spent the time and money getting it
that way. All of these things are possible when you re-direct your
time, thoughts, energy and money away from dealing with clutter
and chaos towards achieving these things. How would that feel?
Feel the feelings that would cause you to feel.

EXERCISE:

WHAT WOULD YOU LOOK LIKE IF YOU HAD AMPLE TIME FOR PERSONAL GROOMING? WHAT WOULD IT BE LIKE TO LOOK LIKE THAT?

_____

_____

_____

4) Stretch your thinking. Add to this list. Think of as many rewards as you can. The more rewards you think of the more motivated you will be to tackle this organizing project.

EXERCISE:

IN WHAT OTHER WAYS WILL IT REWARD YOU PHYSICALLY?

_____

_____

_____

29

Organizing Your Neuro-Associations: Mixed Associations

Now it's time we address your mixed associations. We need to find the ways a disorganized office has been serving you somehow. List 20 positive things you associate with a *disorganized* office. It may be about what that says about the people who inhabit it. It may be about what that means about you. It may be about what other benefits it gives you. It may be about how you don't have to worry about certain things.

EXERCISE:

WHAT ARE THE POSITIVE ASSOCIATIONS YOU HAVE WITH A DISORGANIZED OFFICE? IN OTHER WORDS, WHAT'S GOOD ABOUT LETTING THINGS STAY LESS-ORGANIZED?

Organize Your Office for Success

As long as you have beliefs that keeping things less-organized can be a good thing, you will not be driven to keep things highly organized. You need to write rejection statements that help you deny those beliefs so you can move forward without reservations. Write rejection statements for the 20 positive things you associate to a *disorganized* office. These are statements that start out as; It is not true that... I no longer believe that... I now know that... Replace your positive associations to a *disorganized* office with replacement statements that support an *organized* mindset. Statements that start out as; I now know... I now believe... Now I know it's true that...

EXERCISE:

WHAT ARE THE REJECTION STATEMENTS FOR THE POSITIVE ASSOCIATIONS YOU HAVE WITH A LESS-ORGANIZED OFFICE?

_____

_____

_____

I have led you through an exercise to help you organize your associations. In order for it to create lasting results you need to get into the habit of doing daily mental conditioning. I'll teach you how.

It all begins with the thoughts that are in your conscious and subconscious mind. If the thoughts are empowering, you experience great things in your life. If the thoughts are disempowering, you experience difficulties.

For example my thoughts that financial abundance meant spiritual decay. They totally disempowered my ability to create financial security and they didn't improve my spirituality either. They were disempowering thoughts.

Back in my cluttered days I had thoughts that highly organized people were just anal. It was very difficult for me to be motivated to get organized with those thoughts filling my head and nervous system. It left me desperately disorganized for many years.

Organize Your Office for Success

Can you control or take charge of your thoughts? Negative messages are everywhere. Sometimes thoughts pop into your mind without your intending them to. You're not even aware of your subconscious thoughts. Fortunately for us, there has been extensive research and development on thought management. Discoveries have been made about how our conscious and subconscious mind works.

For a free download of our special report "25 Quick Tips to Finally Get Control of Your Messy Environment" visit: www.OrganizeEnterprise.com/25quicktips.

30

Your Conscious and Subconscious Mind

Your conscious mind acts as a decision maker. It questions everything. It looks at every thought, idea, or image that comes in and decides if it is true or false, good or bad. It can decide to avoid exposure to that which is false or harmful, and acts as a guard to protect the subconscious mind. The subconscious mind does not question anything. It simply accepts everything that comes in as a goal to be acquired. Every thought, idea or image both good and bad approaches your conscious mind. Your conscious mind *decides* to allow it thus exposing your subconscious mind to it or protecting the subconscious from harm.

You can visualize your conscious mind as a great warrior with a steel helmet, breastplate, sword and shield protecting its muscular frame. This warrior stands guard over two doors that lead to your subconscious mind. One door is made of gold and is the entry for every empowering thought, idea, or image. The other door is black and foreboding and is the entry for every disempowering thought, idea, or image. Each and every thought/image approaches this great warrior standing guard over the two doors. The warrior looks at the thought/image carefully as it approaches. Before the thought/image completely arrives, the warrior uses its strength to make one of three decisions. Either it decides it is something that should go in the gold door and opens the gold door for it to pass through or it decides it is something that should go in the black door and it opens the black door and lets it pass through or it decides it is something that it does not want to pass through either door, and stands guard at the doors making sure the thought/image is not allowed to pass. It decides to take action so the mind is not exposed to that thought, idea or image. If the warrior fails to keep the doors shut by avoiding all exposure to that which is disempowering, harmful, negative, and ugly, then those harmful thoughts, ideas, and images enter the subconscious mind and if they are your dominant thought the subconscious mind goes to work to make them your reality. If the conscious mind decides to keep the gold door open by exposing the subconscious mind to thoughts that are empowering, helpful, positive and beautiful on a regular basis, then the subconscious works to make those things your reality.

Have you ever watched a video scene so disturbing that you decided you didn't want to put that kind of stuff in your mind so you got up and turned the video off? That was your conscious mind deciding not to allow those thoughts or images to be exposed to the subconscious mind. Have you ever caught yourself thinking negative thoughts about someone and chose to focus instead on what was good about that person? That was your conscious mind deciding to cast out those negative thoughts and allow in positive thoughts.

Notice I didn't say that your conscious mind could decide to allow those thoughts or images to enter your mind on the conscious level, but not go on to your subconscious level. If it is not immediately cast out of your conscious mind – meaning that you choose not to be exposed to it – the thought automatically proceeds to your subconscious mind. So every book you read, movie you watch, conversation or song you listen to, or *doubt or fear* you think about enters your subconscious mind. It is perceived as a goal you want to have manifested in your life. *If it remains the dominant thought or belief,* your subconscious cannot rest until the thought or belief becomes a reality.

Lynea Corson, Ph.D in Psycho-Educational Processes and certified Transactional Therapist, in her book The Secrets of Super Selling How to Program Your Subconscious for Success offers a challenge. She suggests that "if you doubt the power of radio, television, movies, videos, cassettes, compact discs, newspapers, magazines, and signs, you might want to try the following experiment. For a week watch and listen only to programs that are frightening, sad, angry, etc. Then be aware of your daily thoughts and feelings. For the next week, watch and listen only to programs that deal with happiness, success, and accomplishment. Be aware of your thoughts and feelings during this time also. See for yourself if there is a difference in the way you think and feel, and in the results you achieve. (To get a stronger appreciation for how negative and positive programming play a part in your life, try the experiment for a longer period of time.)"

Your subconscious mind

"Maxwell Maltz wrote in his book, Psycho-Cybernetics that what is often called the subconscious mind is not really a mind at all. It is a wonderful goal striving mechanism made up of the brain and nervous system. The goals that it seeks to achieve are the mental images you have created in your imagination." It sees any image you hold in your imagination as a goal that must be achieved. It absorbs every thought or image it receives. It *remembers* everything it has *ever* received. It works day and night to make those goals a reality. It works relentlessly to manifest those outcomes in your life. It literally takes images that were formed by the thoughts you think and turns them into realities. Your subconscious mind cannot tell what is real and what is not real. It assumes that everything your conscious mind allows in is real. If there are conflicting thoughts, your subconscious will manifest the most dominant thought. The dominant thoughts are the thoughts that have been repeated the most. The dominant thoughts are the thoughts your nervous system has the strongest "feelings" about.

You experience a problem when you allow your warrior (the conscious mind) to become lazy. In other words you stop looking at every thought or image to determine if it is a thought you want to allow in or a thought you want to cast out. Your warrior rests at the side, allowing everything to pass through the black door so you don't have to go to the effort of scrutinizing everything.

If this is the case, your conscious and subconscious mind becomes *cluttered* with disempowering thoughts. *I don't have time for that. I hate doing that. I'm no good at that.* Perhaps the clutter of disempowering thoughts has become so deep or chaotic you are not able to function at your best. Perhaps you have empowering thoughts, but they are not accessible or easy to refer to. *I can. I will.* You need to clear out disempowering thoughts and beliefs.

You need to implement systems that help you access empowering thoughts and beliefs whenever you need them. Organizing your mind is no different than organizing your filing system. You may not enjoy the process. You may even have doubts as to whether the process works or not. However, there are organizing principles that stand true whether *you* do them or not. There is only one way to get the results you want and that is…to be *willing* to follow the principle-based organizing process to organize your conscious and subconscious mind to get those results.

31

Organizing Your Mind

You can shape an environment in your mind that will support you in achieving the level of productivity you desire. That level of productivity allows you to achieve your greatest career goals. First, let's examine the principles of your subconscious mind so you understand how it works, so you are able to use it to your advantage and avoid using it to your disadvantage.

It's better to think of organizing your mind as a type of conditioning instead of a type of programming. It is not something you can just program in your mind once and expect lasting change. Mental conditioning is just like physical conditioning. A physical muscle starts out small and grows bigger and better over time. Your ability to condition your mind and produce results starts out small, but it grows bigger and better over time. The conditioning needs to be a daily event. The principles of your subconscious mind are as follows:

Organize Your Office for Success

Your subconscious mind needs your goals to be precise, and it works to obtain exactly what you think about.

Your subconscious pursues whatever mental images are in your imagination. Those images are developed in your imagination as thoughts are entered into your mind. The thoughts you enter into your mind need to be precise and exactly what you want. If you want to program your subconscious to reach a goal such as boosting your productivity, you need to give it precise instructions. Such as:

- "I increase business profits an extra 20% every year."

- "I spend the first three hours of every day producing new product."

- "I maintain an organized, clutter-free office, mind, and schedule so I free up more space and time to pursue my goals."

- "I streamline my email responses."

- "I effectively delegate ___% of the work that flows into my office."

- "I handle interruptions in 60 seconds or I schedule them into my calendar."

- "Each evening I prioritize my work for the following day."

- "I work on my <u>top</u> priorities all day."

Precise instructions such as these will help you boost your productivity with ease and speed. Because your subconscious mind works to obtain *exactly* what you say you want, you must be very careful and exact in your wording. Your subconscious does not calculate what you *mean* by your thoughts. It takes your thoughts as literal truths, so you must use exact wording of what you truly want. It would be a mistake to think, "I boost my productivity so I can get everything done." Your subconscious mind doesn't know exactly what you want. You may boost your productivity by .000000001% every two years. You may get demoted or fired so you don't have very much that needs to get done. Give exact details of your goal such as, "I complete the Johnston project by January 1, 2007 and I do it working only 30 hours a week." Your subconscious mind will know exactly *how much* to boost your productivity. It will know exactly *how often* or *how quickly* to do it.

Drake wanted to expand his business. At first his goal was to expand his business by 25%. After giving careful consideration to the precision of his goals he set the goal of opening a second office in Las Vegas and landing a million dollar contract by the State of Nevada within 3 years.

As a goal seeking mechanism your subconscious mind works just as hard to create negative conditions that you imagine as it does to create positive conditions that you imagine. If you think about your dreams, goals and positive affirmations, your subconscious mind will work to make those manifest in your life. If you think of doubts, worries, or fears, your subconscious mind will work to make those manifest in your life. If you think of both your dreams and your doubts, your subconscious will pursue whatever is the most dominant thought. Whichever thought has the most feeling energy connected to it.

Drake set a goal of finding a competent manager for his second office but he had fears that he would never find someone who could meet the criteria he was looking for. Drake had confidence that his fears would be manifest rather than his goal. Drake struggled to find a manager.

Your subconscious mind acts on whatever happens to be the most dominant thought.

If you have hopes of becoming more productive, but you also believe that increased productivity will never happen because there are too many things working against you, your subconscious will work to achieve whichever is the most dominant thought. If you have hopes of achieving your career goals, but you also have fears that they won't be realized, your subconscious will work to achieve whichever thought is the most dominant. The most dominant thought is the thought that has the most power and conviction. It's the thought that has been repeated the most often and the one you see most clearly in your mind. It's the thought in which you have the strongest belief that is true and the one you feel the most strongly about.

Drake took an assessment of his fears. He recognized he was defeating himself because his fears were his most dominant thoughts. He practiced mental conditioning every day with rejection statements such as "I no longer believe I'll have difficulty finding a manager who can meet the criteria I'm looking for." He created replacement statements such as, "I now know I will easily find a competent manager within the next two months. I know there are people who exceed my expectations and I know one will be interested in my management position." Drake visualized his fears dissolving and his goal materializing. He spent time each day feeling hope, anticipation, trust, confidence and excitement about finding his manager. By doing this Drake changed his most dominant thought away from his fears and toward his goal of finding a manager.

Your subconscious mind needs the thoughts or goals repeated over and over.

You can visualize how the subconscious mind works if you picture a map with a zillion roads that have been laid just one thin strand at a time. Every time you have an experience, your subconscious looks through its "map" and finds an experience/road that is similar. Then it lays another strand on that road/experience, making it bigger and stronger. Making it more *dominant!* Your subconscious does not know if the experience was real or merely imagined. It accepts every image that comes into your mind as a real experience, whether you put the image there on purpose or not. Your subconscious works to achieve the biggest, strongest, and most dominant roads/experiences you tell it to achieve.

Drake developed the habit of doing his mental conditioning every morning when he first arose and every evening before he went to sleep at night. He had his goals, rejection statements and replacement statements recorded on an audio cassette that he listened to every morning and evening. That way the exact same thoughts and pictures were established in his mind at least twice a day every day until they were manifested in his life.

Your subconscious mind, a goal seeking mechanism, helps you get whatever you see in your imagination (the picture you see in your minds eye). The most dominant images in your imagination are determined by what you believe. Remember, your subconscious mind does not record thoughts. It records the images that the thoughts create. You think thoughts. Those thoughts form images in your mind. Those images are recorded in your subconscious mind as something to be achieved. You can also look at pictures to plant images for your subconscious mind to achieve. In fact, looking at a picture repeatedly speeds up the process, because you see the exact same image every single time. Seeing the exact same image every time gives your subconscious a very clear target to aim for. Looking at it repeatedly lays strands on your subconscious' map and makes it the most dominant thought.

However, no matter what you *believe* you want to attain, the picture your subconscious mind creates can counteract the effect. Your beliefs lay more strands on your subconscious map than looking at the picture does. There is far more "feeling energy" attached to the images your beliefs create. So the most dominant images in your imagination are determined by what you believe. Say you were to look at a picture of yourself sitting in a plush executive office. The door plaque has your name on it and has the word "President" underneath it. Now, say you were to look at this picture every day, but you were to *believe* on a deeper level that it would never happen because you are in a family owned business, but you are not a member of the "family." The images in your mind, created by the beliefs in your imagination, would have more energy attached to them. They would remain the dominant image. Your subconscious would go to work to manifest the beliefs in your life instead of the picture you were looking at. This is why you need to become aware of what your beliefs are. You need to clear out unwanted beliefs and replace them with wanted beliefs. There will be more about how to do this a little later in the chapter.

Drake knew there would be a lot of obstacles to his realizing his goal of landing a million dollar contract from the State of Nevada but he firmly believed it would happen within the appointed time. Although concerns came to Drake's mind when he thought about the possibilities he had such a firm belief that he would get the contract. That belief was much stronger then the concerns and it enabled the subconscious to create that reality.

The energy from your feelings is needed for your subconscious to be able to create what you desire.

Your feelings fuel the flame that burns the images into your subconscious. Let's use the analogy of a cigarette lighter. When you strike the flint of the lighter, you get a little spark. If there is no fuel left in the lighter, the spark is all you will get. There is no flame no matter how many times you strike the flint. However, if there is plenty of fuel in the lighter and you strike the flint, you get a flame that you can use to burn what you want. That is how it works in conditioning your subconscious. Looking at an image is like striking the flint. Seeing the image in your subconscious mind produces a spark. Without the fuel of *feelings* the spark is all you will get. There is no flame no matter how many times you look at the image. There is only spark. However, if there are strong feelings, providing plenty of fuel for the image as you look at it, you get an amazing flame. That flame burns the desired outcome deep into your subconscious mind. Whichever image is backed by the biggest flame is the dominant image or the dominant thought.

When Drake did his daily mental conditioning he looked at a tangible picture of his goal, listened to his audio cassette repeating his goals, rejection statements, and replacement statements. He stopped the tape and using his physiology (the way he breathed, carried himself, moved) and his questions (impacting his emotional state by asking empowering questions) and his imagination to fill his system with emotions of hope, anticipation, complete confidence, excitement, joy, gratitude and admiration. Drake stayed in those states for as long as he could as he looked closely at his tangible pictures. Then Drake started the tape again and continued the process with his other goals.

Once a goal is established in your subconscious mind it will continue to make that goal a reality in your life. The only way to stop it from producing that reality is to dissolve it from your subconscious mind.

If you condition your subconscious to produce a certain result, and if, after you produce that result, you decide you want to produce an even better result, you will need to dissolve the original result you programmed into your subconscious. You will need to condition the even better result into your subconscious. Otherwise, you will not see any improvement.

The way to dissolve dominant thoughts is to program specific statements that reject those dominant thoughts. Statements such as, "I no longer believe…" or "It is not true that …" Follow those *rejection statements* with *replacement statements*. Replacement statements are thoughts you prefer to replace them with. Thoughts such as, "I now believe…" or "I now know it is true that… ."

For the first six months that Drake started doing daily mental conditioning he affirmed over and over again, "I earn $150,000 a year working only 40 hours a week." Drake soon had these goals realized. He decided to go for an even higher goal but he continued to earn approximately $150,000 a year. Drake needed to dissolve his old goal and establish a new goal. He needed to condition his subconscious with a new rejection statement and replacement statement. He started daily mental conditioning by affirming, "I no longer earn $150,000 a year working 40 hours a week. I now earn $200,000 a year working only 30 hours a week." By dissolving the old conditioning and replacing it with his new conditioning he was able to reach even higher goals.

In order for your subconscious mind to solve problems or cause achievement, it needs incubation time.

Your subconscious mind needs your conscious mind to program the thoughts and images it needs into your subconscious mind, so it can go to work on them. Your subconscious mind then needs your conscious mind to relax on the matter completely. Your subconscious needs incubation time to solve problems or to achieve your goals. When it is ready it will present its solution or idea to your conscious mind.

If you want ideas to come to you, program into your subconscious what you need by consciously thinking about it. Then forget about it. Spend some time doing activity that doesn't require a lot of mental concentration. That way, your subconscious can notify your conscious mind of its ideas and solutions promptly and easily.

Drake loved to work in the yard. It was very therapeutic for him. He found it worked well for him to clarify what the problem was and what solution was needed and then forget about it and spend time working in his yard. Often times the solution would pop into Drakes mind as he trimmed the hedges or watered the flower beds.

Your subconscious mind has no concept of time. There is no past, present or future. There is only now.

There are no rules as to how long it takes your subconscious mind to achieve the results you are looking for. The subconscious mind has no concept of time. It could take a month, a week, a day, or even an hour to manifest the desired outcome in your life. The amount of time required is determined by what you truly believe is possible and how intensely you desire the result.

What do you want to have in your subconscious mind?

You should have already identified your career/business goals. Be sure you also identify specific goals for your desired level of organization and productivity. Organize your thoughts and beliefs so your subconscious mind can easily achieve your goals. Start by closely examining what is already in your belief systems. Identify any unwanted thoughts or beliefs and cast them out through the use of *rejection statements.*

Remember the previously mentioned example where Drake practiced mental conditioning every day with rejection statements such as "I no longer believe I'll have difficulty finding a manager who can meet the criteria I'm looking for."

To recognize what thoughts and beliefs you have about your goal, write down everything that comes into your mind. Include positive and negative thoughts. Search your mind for any doubts, fears or disbeliefs. Put your pen to the paper and just keep writing. Do not scrutinize the validity of your thoughts, doubts, fears or disbeliefs. That is irrelevant. Let your thoughts flow. Write it all down. Something about writing it on paper forces you to slow your thought processes down to the point that you can think clearly and concisely.

Organize Your Office for Success

Write your desired goal. Write it clear enough for a five year old to understand. An example of this might be, "I get an extra two hours worth of work accomplished each day. I do it without having to spend any extra time at the office."

Before your mind can accept new beliefs, it needs the old beliefs cleared out of the way. You accomplish that by writing rejection statements. A rejection statement is a statement that rejects your old belief or your old, unwanted reality. Write out your rejection statements clearly enough that a five year old could understand them. An example of this would be, "I no longer believe it's difficult to get anything done when there are so many interruptions."

After you have determined the specific characteristics of your goals and you have written out your unwanted thoughts and rejection statements for those unwanted thoughts, you need to design replacement statements that you want conditioned into your subconscious mind instead. Be careful that the replacement statements define what you want as your _final_ result. Write it as if you have already achieved it. Be as specific and clear as you can. An example may be, "I now handle interruptions by asking myself, "Is this interruption more important than what I'm working on, or is what I'm working on more important than this interruption? I always spend my time working on what's most important."

Also, any time there is a delay in achieving your career/business, productivity, or organizing goals, take inventory of your thoughts and beliefs about them and organize them according to the following process. Clarify your goals and your disempowering thoughts or beliefs. Write rejection statements to dissolve those thoughts or beliefs. Write a replacement statement you want to condition into your subconscious.

Drake set the business goal to open a second office in Las Vegas and land a million dollar contract from the State of Nevada within three years. Choose a career or business goal you want to pursue. It could be an increase to your net income. It could be a desire to grow your client base. It could be a new product line you want to develop. Choose a business goal that is meaningful to you.

Now identify your thoughts or beliefs about that goal by writing down everything that pops into your mind when you think about that goal.

Organize Your Office for Success

This is the exercise where you put your pen to paper and let it flow with anything that pops into your mind. That is how you identify what your thoughts and beliefs are.

EXERCISE:

WHAT ARE YOUR CAREER/BUSINESS GOALS?

_____

_____

_____

_____

_____

Drake wrote down every thought that entered his mind when he thought about his goal to open a second office and land the big contract. His paper looked like this.

"I'm going to have to work harder. That will double my income. I can install the pool in the back yard. I may not be able to find a competent manager for the office. That is an awfully large contract to land where Nevada doesn't even know me or my firm. There will be a lot of expenses associated to opening the second office. Perhaps one day my business will be a national company. I will have less time with my family because I will be traveling to Las Vegas often. I'll be able to retire in style if I have two successful offices in two separate states. The economy in Las Vegas is better than in Salt Lake City. My business will really take off. I'll need to hire more people."

Next, reject those unwanted thoughts, doubts, fears and disbeliefs about your career/business by writing rejection statements. (I no longer believe…) (It is not true that…)

Drake looked at his page of thoughts. He circled all the thoughts that were negative or disempowering. He wrote rejection statements for each negative or disempowering thought. His next page looked like this.

Organize Your Office for Success

"I no longer believe that I'm going to have to work harder. It's not true that I may not be able to find a competent manager for the office. I no longer believe that a million dollar contract is too large of contract to land where Nevada doesn't even know me or my firm. I am no longer concerned with the expenses associated to opening the second office. It's not true that I will have less time with my family because I will be traveling to Las Vegas often. I no longer believe it will be a problem to hire more people."

Replace those rejection statements with replacement statements. Statements you now want to have conditioned into your subconscious mind.

Drake wrote a page consisting of his goals, his rejection statements and his replacement statements. His page looked something like this.

"I successfully open a second office in Las Vegas. I land a million dollar contract from the State of Nevada by January 1st, 2010. "I no longer believe that I'm going to have to work harder if I want to accomplish that. I now know that I can work smarter instead of harder. I can leverage myself so not all the workload rests on my shoulders. It's not true that I may not be able to find a competent manager for the office. It is true that I easily find the manager for the office who will meet my needs. I no longer believe that a million dollar contract is too large of contract to land where Nevada doesn't even know me or my firm. I now know that the State of Nevada assigns much larger contracts than that and three years is plenty of time to get my firm established and well known in the State of Nevada. I am no longer concerned with the expenses associated to opening the second office. I now know that the second office will produce profits that far outweigh any expenses. I now know its expensive to go without opening the office in Las Vegas. It's not true that I will have less time with my family because I will be traveling to Las Vegas often. I now know I can create family bonding by having my family travel with me and by making quality time at home when I am home. I no longer believe it will be a problem to hire more people." I now believe there are more competent people looking for work than I have work to provide. I can easily recruit and train the people I need to reach my goal."

Fears About Achieving My
Business Goals

WHAT ARE THE THOUGHTS, DOUBTS, FEARS, AND BELIEFS YOU
HAVE ABOUT THESE GOALS BEING REALIZED?

_____

_____

_____

_____

Rejection Statements

WRITE REJECTION STATEMENTS FOR ALL THE NEGATIVE OR
DISEMPOWERING THOUGHTS YOU HAD ABOUT REACHING YOUR
CAREER OR BUSINESS GOALS

_____

_____

_____

_____

Replacement Statements

WRITE REPLACEMENT STATEMENTS FOR EACH OF THE
REJECTION STATEMENTS. THESE WILL BE THE STATEMENTS YOU
NOW WANT TO HAVE CONDITIONED INTO YOUR SUBCONSCIOUS
MIND

_____

_____

_____

_____

EXERCISE:

WRITE A SPECIFIC GOAL, A REJECTION STATEMENT AND A REPLACEMENT STATEMENT FOR ALL THE NEGATIVE OR DISEMPOWERING THOUGHTS YOU HAD ABOUT REACHING YOUR CAREER OR BUSINESS GOAL.

Career/Business Goals:

Very Specific Goal: _____

Rejection Statement: _____

Replacement Statement: _____

Very Specific Goal: _____

Rejection Statement: _____

Replacement Statement: _____

Very Specific Goal: _____

Rejection Statement: _____

Replacement Statement: _____

Very Specific Goal: _____

Rejection Statement: _____

Replacement Statement: _____

Very Specific Goal: _____

Rejection Statement: _____

Replacement Statement: _____

Organize Your Office for Success

Now do the same process for your productivity goals. A productivity goal is a goal of what you are able to produce within an allotted time. For example your productivity goal may be to complete your assignments 48 hours before they are due without having to work overtime. Another productivity goal may be to complete nine projects every month as opposed to the four projects you have been able to complete up to this point. You can set productivity goals that are more specific such as writing five pages of your manuscript per day, making 20 phone calls per hour, or processing 10 tasks per hour.

Drake set some productivity goals. His goals were to prepare and submit four proposals a month, complete projects by their deadline without having to work overtime, and meet with two qualified manager candidates a week.

EXERCISE:

WHAT ARE YOUR PRODUCTIVITY GOALS?

_____

_____

_____

_____

_____

_____

Now identify your thoughts or beliefs about that goal by writing down everything that pops into your mind when you think about that goal. This is the exercise where you put your pen to paper and let it flow with anything that pops into your mind. That is how you identify what your thoughts and beliefs are.

Drake got out his pen and paper. He wrote down every thought that came into his mind when he considered his productivity goal of completing projects by their deadline without having to work overtime. His page looked something like this.

"I know better. It is going to take a lot of overtime to complete the projects on time. My customers would be happier. The only way we'll avoid   working a lot of overtime is to hire more people and that is expensive. This is going to be hard. We'd develop a better reputation. I'll have to accept fewer projects and that will decrease my income. Maybe I can learn to do more in less time. I need an administrative assistant. I'm too stressed out trying to produce so much without increasing the amount of time I have to work on the projects."

Reject those unwanted thoughts, doubts, fears and disbeliefs about your productivity by writing rejection statements. (I no longer believe…) (It is not true that…)

Drake wrote the following rejection statements for his disempowering thoughts.

"It is not true that it is going to take a lot of overtime to complete projects on time. I no longer believe that the only way we'll avoid working a lot of overtime is to hire more people. It is not true that hiring more people is too expensive. I no longer believe that this is going to be hard. It's not true that I'll have to accept fewer projects. It's not true that accepting fewer projects will decrease my income. I no longer believe I'll be stressed out trying to produce more in less time."

Replace those rejection statements with replacement statements. Statements you now want to have conditioned into your subconscious mind. A replacement statement is most commonly known as a positive affirmation.

Drake wrote a page consisting of his goals, his rejection statements and his replacement statements. His page looked something like this.

"I complete projects by their deadline without having to work overtime. " It is not true that it is going to take a lot of overtime to complete projects on time. It is true that we receive training on how to produce more in less time and we implement what we learn. I now know it is true that we complete the projects by their deadline

without working overtime. I no longer believe that the only way we'll avoid working a lot of overtime is to hire more people. I now know that each of us can develop skills to be more productive. It is not true that hiring more people is too expensive. I now know that hiring more people will generate more income that will exceed the expenses. I no longer believe that this is going to be hard. I now know it will be very do-able. It's not true that I'll have to accept fewer projects. It's not true that accepting fewer projects will decrease my income. I now know I can increase my fees per project so I earn the same amount of money without taking on the extra projects. I no longer believe I'll be stressed out trying to produce more in less time. I now know producing more in less time will minimize my stress."

Fears About Achieving My Productivity Goals

WHAT ARE THE THOUGHTS, DOUBTS, FEARS, AND BELIEFS YOU HAVE ABOUT THESE GOALS BEING REALIZED?

_____

_____

_____

_____

Rejection Statements

WRITE REJECTION STATEMENTS FOR ALL THE NEGATIVE OR DISEMPOWERING THOUGHTS YOU HAD ABOUT REACHING YOUR CAREER OR BUSINESS GOALS

_____

_____

_____

_____

Replacement Statements

WRITE REPLACEMENT STATEMENTS FOR EACH OF THE REJECTION STATEMENTS. THESE WILL BE THE STATEMENTS YOU NOW WANT TO HAVE CONDITIONED INTO YOUR SUBCONSCIOUS MIND

_____

_____

_____

_____

EXERCISE:
WRITE A SPECIFIC GOAL, A REJECTION STATEMENT AND A
REPLACEMENT STATEMENT FOR ALL THE NEGATIVE OR
DISEMPOWERING THOUGHTS YOU HAD ABOUT REACHING
YOUR PRODUCTIVITY GOALS.

Productivity Goals:

Very Specific Goal: _____

Rejection Statement: _____

Replacement Statement: _____

Very Specific Goal: _____

Rejection Statement: _____

Replacement Statement: _____

Very Specific Goal: _____

Rejection Statement: _____

Replacement Statement: _____

Very Specific Goal: _____

Rejection Statement: _____

Replacement Statement: _____

Very Specific Goal: _____

Rejection Statement: _____

Replacement Statement: _____

Very Specific Goal: _____

Rejection Statement: _____

Replacement Statement: _____

Finally follow the same process for your getting organized goals. Lets revisit my definition of being organized at the office.

- To be organized at the office means you have everything established so you function at your very best, feel great about the way your space and work looks, and so your level of productivity is congruent with your work demands or ambitions.

- To be organized at the office means you have your career goals clearly established in your mind and you have mastered the mental conditioning that drives you to reach those goals.

- To be organized at the office means to have a master plan of what activities will produce the outcomes you desire, have work stations set up to perform those activities, and to have the equipment and supplies that are needed in their appropriate place.

- To be organized at the office means to eliminate the clutter in your office space. It means to eliminate the clutter that runs amuck in your mind. It means to eliminate the clutter that fills your schedule.

- To be organized at the office means you have organized your thoughts, beliefs, what you associate pleasure and pain to, your feelings, and behaviors so they work together to propel you to success.

- To be organized at the office means to have a structured schedule where activities are compressed and organized in a manner that enables you to perform at the height of efficiency and effectiveness. It means you have structured behaviors such as habits and routines that help you be efficient and effective in your work.

- To be organized at the office means to implement systems that minimize your stress and increase your work capacity. It's having systems so well established that you can go on automatic pilot so you can concentrate on your projects not your process. These systems should be set up in such a way that they require the minimum amount of maintenance.

- To be organized at the office means to have a work process flow where work flows into your office, gets processed efficiently and effectively in your office and flows out of your office in a timely manner.

- To be organized at the office means you master management skills. Management of time, task, team, space, information, paperwork, email, interruptions, meetings, delegation, discarding, prioritizing, processing, scheduling, etc. etc. etc.

Drake looked at the above definition and he set some goals for himself of mastering the skills of effective delegation and follow up, keeping his desk clear of everything except the project he was currently working on, and processing his work through a new work processing system.

Now look at the above definition and determine some goals you want to work on so you are better organized at the office.

Now identify your thoughts or beliefs about that goal by writing down everything that pops into your mind when you think about that goal. This is the exercise where you put your pen to paper and let it flow with anything that pops into your mind. That is how you identify what your thoughts and beliefs are.

EXERCISE:

WHAT ARE YOUR PRODUCTIVITY GOALS?

_____

_____

_____

_____

_____

_____

Drake got out his pen and paper. He wrote down every thought that came into his mind when he considered his "getting organized" goals of mastering the skills of effective delegation and follow up. His page looked something like this.

"I'll have to rely on other people and other people are not reliable. I may get into big trouble if something needs to be done and the other people don't come through. People may resent that I'm unloading my work onto them. I'll really free up a lot of time by delegating the bulk of my work. How do I follow up without making my people feel like I'm micro-managing? I only have two people I can delegate to. Delegation never really works. It always breaks down in the process. Things get lost or forgotten. I guess when I'm honest with myself I don't really believe other people can do as good of a job as I can do so I'd rather do it myself so I stay in control."

Reject those unwanted thoughts, doubts, fears and disbeliefs about your ability to get organized by writing rejection statements. (I no longer believe…) (It is not true that…)

Drake wrote rejection statements for his disempowering thoughts.

"I no longer have concerns about relying on other people. I no longer believe that people are unreliable. It's not true that my people won't come through when something needs to be done. I no longer believe that people may resent that I'm unloading my work onto them. I no longer worry about how to follow up without making my people feel like I'm micro-managing? It's not true that I only have two people I can delegate to. I no longer believe that delegation never really works. I no longer believe that it always breaks down in the process or that things get lost or forgotten. It's not true that other people can't do as good of a job as I can do. I no longer feel like I'd rather do it myself because I no longer believe it is necessary in order to stay in control."

Replace those rejection statements with replacement statements. Statements you now want to have conditioned into your subconscious mind.

Drake wrote a page consisting of his goals, his rejection statements and his replacement statements. His page looked something like this.

"I master the skills of effective delegation and follow up. I no longer have concerns about relying on other people. I no longer believe that people are unreliable. I now know that good people are reliable people   and I have good people on my team. It's not true that my people won't come through when something needs to be done. It is

true that my people come through every time. I no longer believe that people may resent that I'm unloading my work onto them. I now know that everyone appreciates that is how the work gets done and we all pitch in to contribute to the greater good. I no longer worry about how to follow up without making my people feel like I'm micro-managing. I now know a system of accountability and follow up is the only way to successfully delegate. I no longer believe that delegation never really works. I now know that once we establish an effective delegation cycle that the cycle will work beautifully every time. I no longer believe that it always breaks down in the process or that things get lost or forgotten. I now know I have an effective follow up system that eliminates the possibility of things getting lost or forgotten. It's not true that other people can't do as good of a job as I can do. I now believe I have competent people who are capable and dependable to do just as good of a job as I can. I no longer feel like I'd rather do it myself so I stay in control. I now know its possible for me to stay in control without having to do everything myself.

Fears About Achieving My
Getting Organized Goals

WHAT ARE THE THOUGHTS, DOUBTS, FEARS, AND BELIEFS YOU HAVE ABOUT THESE GOALS BEING REALIZED?

_____

_____

_____

_____

Rejection Statements

WRITE REJECTION STATEMENTS FOR ALL THE NEGATIVE OR DISEMPOWERING THOUGHTS YOU HAD ABOUT REACHING YOUR CAREER OR BUSINESS GOALS

_____

_____

_____

_____

Replacement Statements

WRITE REPLACEMENT STATEMENTS FOR EACH OF THE REJECTION STATEMENTS. THESE WILL BE THE STATEMENTS YOU NOW WANT TO HAVE CONDITIONED INTO YOUR SUBCONSCIOUS MIND

_____

_____

_____

_____

EXERCISE:
WRITE A SPECIFIC GOAL, A REJECTION STATEMENT AND A REPLACEMENT STATEMENT FOR ALL THE NEGATIVE OR DISEMPOWERING THOUGHTS YOU HAD ABOUT REACHING YOUR "GETTING ORGANIZED GOALS.

Getting Organized Goals:

Very Specific Goal: _____

Rejection Statement: _____

Replacement Statement: _____

Very Specific Goal: _____

Rejection Statement: _____

Replacement Statement: _____

Very Specific Goal: _____

Rejection Statement: _____

Replacement Statement: _____

Very Specific Goal: _____

Rejection Statement: _____

Replacement Statement: _____

Very Specific Goal: _____

Rejection Statement: _____

Replacement Statement: _____

Very Specific Goal: _____

Rejection Statement: _____

Replacement Statement: _____

It is painful and not likely that people will behave contrary to the identity they hold for themselves. Just as important as checking your thoughts, beliefs, associations, feelings, and behaviors is checking the identity of the person you see yourself as. The bottom line is this: You will inevitably do anything and sacrifice everything to live a life that is consistent with the identity you hold for yourself. Create an identity that is empowering, using the same methods you used to condition your subconscious mind. Look for the negative or the disempowering identity traits. Cast them out using rejection statements. Replace them with positive or empowering replacement statements.

Another part of clearing out unwanted thoughts and mental images is avoiding negative conditioning. Carefully monitor the media you watch, listen to, or participate in. You want to carefully monitor conversations, wandering thoughts or imagination, images or influences that cause your conscious mind to think and imagine negative consequences.

Finally, from time to time you will want to ascertain if there are any roadblocks in achieving your desired outcomes. Roadblocks may come in the form of thoughts, beliefs, associations, feelings, behaviors, or results. You want to seek out negatives. Dissolve them from your subconscious mind through rejection statements. Replace them with positive replacement statements.

You want to boost your productivity and experience greater career success. That is why you have picked up this book and are reading it. Success will be manifested in your life *if* you control and direct your thoughts. You can create your preferred dominant thoughts and control what your subconscious mind sees as the goals to achieve through daily mental conditioning. Specifics on how to do daily mental conditioning are included a little later in the book. If you do the daily mental conditioning, your desired level of productivity and success *will* become your literal reality.

Audio Recordings

Beyond clearing out the unwanted thoughts, organize and submit the *wanted* thoughts into your subconscious mind. Create an audio recording of your goals, rejection statements, and replacement statements so you condition into your subconscious the same message day after day. Update your audio recording every month or so. To create your audio recording, do the following:

- Write a goal you feel strongly about.

- Consider all the thoughts and feelings you have about that goal. Include both good and bad thoughts and feelings. Both empowering and disempowering. Write them all down.

- Under the goal, write rejection statements and replacement statements for your disempowering thoughts, beliefs, and feelings.

- Under the rejection and replacement statements, write statements for the empowering thoughts you already have about the goal. You want them to be included in your conditioning.

- Make an audio recording of your goals, rejection statements, and replacement statements.

- Listen to your audio recording daily.

- Update your recording as needed.

Monique wanted to establish her reputation as one of the most productive, efficient, and effective members of the staff. She made an audio recording and listened to it every day. The audio recording included the following: *I have established myself as the most productive member of the team. I no longer believe that I'll have to work long hours to maintain such a reputation. I now believe that I have mastered the skills that will help me produce the most work without spending extra time. I no longer believe that my efforts will be underappreciated. I now believe I will receive great opportunities due to my diligence in producing high results. I am the most productive member of the entire staff.* Monique rose through the ranks of the office due to her impressive reputation for being such a high producer.

Edmund wanted to maintain an organized office. He made an audio recording and listened to it every day. The audio recording included the following: *I maintain a clutter-free, organized office. It is not true that I won't have enough time to tend to the details that keep my desk free of clutter and my work processes organized. I now know it is true that keeping things clutter-free and organized frees up additional time and space in my day. It is not true that I am just not a very organized person. I now know it is true that organization skills can be learned, and I am very capable of learning them. It is not true that organized people are obsessive and restrictive. I now know it is true that one can be organized enough to function at his very best without becoming obsessive about it. I now know it is true that organization brings freedom, not restriction. My mind is free to create, my time is free to work on what is most important to me, and my schedule is free to do the things I enjoy, as well as to get my work done. I consistently and easily maintain a clutter-free, organized office.* Edmund organized his office and has maintained it for the past two years.

Misti wanted to increase the number of her sales. She made an audio recording and listened to it every day. The audio recording included the following: *I increase the number of my sales by 25% each and every month. I no longer believe I have to make ten telephone calls just to get one appointment scheduled. I now believe I only have to make three telephone calls to get an appointment scheduled. I no longer believe I only close one out of every eight customers. I now believe that I close one out of every five customers. I no longer believe the economy is bad and so sales are low. I now believe that our product solves people's problems and meets their needs. Thus, our product is easy to sell no matter what the economy is doing. I no longer believe everyone has objections that block the sale. I now believe that objections are simply customers asking for more information. I give them that needed information and close the sales. I increase the number of my sales by 25% each and every month.* In a very short time Misti became number one in sales for the entire district.

Tangible pictures

The right side of the brain needs pictures and feelings. Remember, the subconscious mind sees the images you see in your mind as goals to be achieved. It's important that the images be of the *end result* you want, not of the process to get there. You need to choose your method for creating these images. You can simply visualize images that you have created in your own imagination. However, your imagination will create different details and emphases each time you visualize your goals. It will still work for your mental conditioning, but not as well as if you use tangible pictures. Create a tangible picture of your end result, and look at it every day. Tangible pictures allow you to look at the exact same image every single time. It will be easier and faster for your subconscious to recognize *that image* as the dominant thought and the clearly defined target. The following examples are of people who achieved their goals by focusing on the end result:

Brad was the owner and president of a fairly successful mortgage company. He was happy about the success his company had created. He was also bothered by the amount of business he was missing due to poor levels of productivity. Brad took an accounting of how many income opportunities he had missed out on in the past six months due to his poor productivity. He gained a strong desire to get more productive and make the most of future opportunities. Brad created three graphs showing his levels of personal productivity.

Each graph represented a different month. Each month, the levels on his graphs grew higher and higher. The graphs showed improvements on his ability to quickly find what he needed in order to delegate, streamline, prioritize, and act on his priorities as well as to accomplish income-generating activities. The graphs were in vibrant, magnificent colors. Brad copied pictures of himself onto the graphs. This helped him to see that he was the one experiencing the improvements. He also created a picture of a deposit slip for his business checking account. He wrote in an amount that was significantly higher than his current deposits. Brad found a picture of the swimming pool for his back yard that the increased income would provide for his family. Brad took pictures of each of his family members lounging at a pool. He cut them out and pasted them in the picture of the swimming pool he wanted for his home. Every morning when he arrived at work, Brad closed his office door, pulled out his pictures, and visualized what it would be like to achieve his goals. He looked at them until he was filled with feelings of excitement, determination, enjoyment and satisfaction. Then he put his pictures away and went to work to make those images a reality in his life. Within only a few months, Brad's company was making larger bank deposits. Brad watched as the workers dug the hole in his back yard and put in the new pool.

Adrian received a reprimand from her boss for the piles of clutter in her office and for the amount of time it took her to find anything. She

Organize Your Office for Success

had been teased for years by her co-workers about how messy her office was, but now it was seriously threatening her position with the company. Adrian liked her job and really wanted to do better. She found a picture online of a luxurious, clutter-free office. She printed off the picture in full color. She cut out a picture of herself and pasted it behind the desk of her new office picture. She found the best organized file drawer in the company and had a co-worker take a picture of her sitting behind the desk, replacing a file into the highly organized file system. She took a picture of her boss with a great big smile on his face. Each morning Adrian took a few minutes to look at her pictures and imagined what it would be like to be that organized. Later that year, Adrian's boss stopped by her desk to comment on how much better her office space looked. He had a big smile on his face as he praised her for how much more quickly she was able to find things. He encouraged her to keep up the good work.

Antonio was a struggling attorney at a major law firm. He had aspirations of being made a partner in the firm. He didn't know how he was going to do it. He decided to put his subconscious mind to work for him. He found a picture of all the partners together. He took a picture of himself in his best suit. He cut out the picture of himself and pasted it into the picture of the partners so he could see himself as one of that group. He created a full-color certificate of recognition naming him as partner of the firm. He chose the vehicle he would want to drive when he was awarded a company vehicle as one of the benefits of being a partner. He went to the dealership that sold the vehicle he wanted and had the salesman take a picture of him getting into it. He wrote up a feature article announcing his partnership. He inserted it into the local newspaper's business section as if they had run the story. Antonio was afraid someone at work might see his pictures. He kept them at home by his bedside. Each morning when the alarm went off, he sat up in bed and looked at his pictures and imagined his promotion. Antonio was eventually made partner and then senior partner of the firm.

32

What You Accomplish by Mental Conditioning

When you do your mental conditioning on a regular basis, you change the way you think, feel, believe and behave. You'll start to say the right things to create the reality you want. You'll start to do the right things. You'll start to behave in the right manner. The amazing thing is that it also affects the way other people behave. In the same way, a television station sends out a signal that travels through the air waves. That signal is picked up by anyone who has a television and antenna. It is believed that our subconscious minds take the pictures we see in our imaginations and electromagnetically charges them with our energy. It sends out that signal through the air waves much like a television station does. Science has proven that we each have an energy field that is literally light energy. It flows in a circuit, travels through space, and performs work. It pulls to us whatever we picture, and pushes away from us anything different from what we see in our imaginations. The combination of our pictures plus our feelings about them carries our images into the air to be picked up by others.

Daily Conditioning

Set aside a time each day for your mental conditioning. It needs to be a quiet time, when you will not be interrupted or distracted.

Get out your tangible pictures and your audio recording.

Look at your tangible pictures. Imagine you are looking at it with the force of a laser beam.

As you look at your pictures, get into the feelings of pride, hope, excitement, joy, etc. that you will feel once you have achieved your goal. Hold those feelings for at least 30 seconds.

Then, turn on your audio recording about that goal. Your recording should be enthusiastic.

Take time to see your subconscious transmitting your image to the world and the world bringing back to you your goal realized.

Once you have done this, sit quietly for a moment. Allow your subconscious mind to enter ideas into your conscious mind, anything you should say or do today, any place you should be at any time, anything you should be ready for. Insights may come to you in many different ways. It may be something you read or hear. It may be something you think or do. Don't get stuck in the rut of thinking it has to come to you in a particular way or time.

Take time to do your mental conditioning *daily*.

Share your vision

If you are dependant on other people to reach your goal, be sure you share your vision with them. I don't mean share your tangible pictures with them. I just mean that you should explain to them what you are after. It is difficult for your team to hit a target if they can't see it or don't know where it is. Share the vision with everyone concerned and give them some form of daily conditioning to help them stay focused on it. Unite the forces. Together, everyone is better.

Stay true to your course

The ping pong ball analogy illustrates how so many people bounce in different directions every time someone or something makes contact. You will be offered unlimited possibilities of things to do with your time, mind, and resources. It takes a firm resolve to stay true to the course once you determine what course you should take. I recommend that you get into the habit of approaching every person, task, telephone call, etc. with the question in your mind, "Does this take me closer to my goals, or does it merely steer me off course?" Stay true to your course.

The Typical Organized Workday

I want you to visualize a typical day at the office once you get organized. Imagine yourself getting to work and going into your office. Before you visit with other employees, before you check your email or voicemail, and before the phones start to ring, you sit at your desk and pull out your cassette player and your tangible pictures. You focus on your business goals by listening to your recording and by concentrating on your tangible pictures. Imagine yourself putting away the cassette player and pictures when the tape is through. You pull your top-priority task from your inbox and go right to work on it. You make a substantial contribution to the activity that was aligned with your business goals before responding to all the "noise" in the office. You feel great about what you have already accomplished, and it's not even 10 a.m. yet.

Imagine yourself sitting behind your desk. It is completely clear of paper except for the item you are currently working on. You finish that task and quickly file it away. You pull your next prioritized task from your inbox and see that you need the staple remover. Your hand goes to the desk drawer and pulls out the staple remover without you looking, because the staple remover is always in the exact same place.

Working with Your Processing System

Imagine being disciplined enough all day long to run *everything* through your processing system. As tasks flow into your life, you enter them into your system. You gather, filter, prioritize and act. When you complete a task, you go to your tickler file to determine what you are to do next. You never shoot from the hip, responding to every influence (ping pong paddle) in your world. You rely on the tickler file to dictate what you do and when you do it because you have been faithful in properly gathering, filtering, prioritizing and acting. You always know you are spending your time doing the most important activity you could do, since everything was properly processed through your processing system.

Compressing Your Activity

Just like compressing the Legos together created more space in the container, compressing like activities with like activities throughout the day will create more time available during the day. Compressing activities that you can do to free up more time are:

• Resisting the urge to check your emails until the most important projects of the day have been completed.

• Checking your emails only once or twice a day.

• Compressing all your email replies back to back.

• Streamlining verbiage in your emails. Keeping emails as short as possible.

• Standing up when talking on the phone so you are uncomfortable, so as to bring your telephone conversations to a close sooner.

• Making calls just before lunch or just before the end of the day so you can keep them short. Open conversations by saying that you are just on your way out but that you wanted to make a quick call to them.

• Compress all your outgoing telephone calls back to back.

• Compress all your meetings back to back as much as possible.

• Schedule 45-minute meetings instead of one hour meetings.

The End of Each Day

Imagine pulling out the final task from your inbox 30 minutes before closing time. It is your sales report for the month, waiting for your review. You see that sales are up. The improvement in your productivity has really made a difference. You turn to your computer and confirm that your email inbox is empty. You have responded to all of your emails and phone messages. You have delegated and followed up on all appropriate items. No one interrupts you as you pull from your desk file drawer your stack of tasks for you to do tomorrow. You take ten minutes to prioritize tomorrow's tasks. You place the stack in your empty inbox. The top-priority task is sitting on the top of the stack to greet you first thing in the morning. With a sense of control, you turn off the lights and leave the office a few minutes early to beat rush hour traffic.

For a free download of our special report "25 Quick Tips to Finally Get Control of Your Messy Environment" visit: www.OrganizeEnterprise.com/25quicktips.

About the Author

Christi Youd is an organizing consultant, professional speaker and the founder/President of Organize Enterprise. She is responsible for the creation of popular and innovative organization systems available for both home and corporate use.

Featured in publications such as Steven M.R. Covey's *Speed of Trust, New York Times, Martha Stewart Living Magazine, Selling Power.com* and several other publications, Christi is also the celebrated author of *Organize Your Office for Success* and *Organize Your Home in 10 Minutes a Day*. A member of both the National Association of Professional Organizers and the National Speakers Association, Christi is an accomplished yet accessible leader in her field. She transitions easily from coaching business executives to harried homemakers, proving workable, sustainable organizational solutions to restore harmony and productivity in the home or workplace.

Trained by the National Association of Professional Organizers, with 20 years dedicated to research and development, Christi is recognized as a proficient speaker, organizer and author. As a workshop presenter and speaker, she has a reputation for being "personable" and "hilarious" with fun, true-life stories interspersed throughout her lectures.

Christi and her husband Russell are the proud parents of three well-adjusted – and organized! – children. She particularly enjoys her "pet project"; her bi-weekly ezine, "Organized To Succeed", is emailed to subscribers throughout the world. To subscribe to Christi's ezine go to www.OrganizeEnterprise.com/ezinesubscribe

Christi Youd is available for training workshops, speaking engagements, interviews, and private consulting. Send your request via email to: Christi@OrganizeEnterprise.com or call (801)756-3382.

Whatever kind of business you're doing, you can <u>do it better</u> thanks to a revolutionary approach to organization and success. It's a brand new **all-in-one information resource** that can help you <u>**accomplish**</u> <u>*all* **your business goals.**</u>

Christi Youd's Organize Enterprise – Training Wheels for Business

A crash-course in better business organization from Organize Enterprise

An 8-part DVD Training Course that can be customized to your business and employees

For details go to <u>www.OrganizeEnterprise.com/trainingwheels</u> or contact us at (801)756-3382 email <u>Christi@OrganizeEnterprise.com</u>

Book Christi to come to you!

She will train and organize your team in her amazing three-day program.

At the conclusion of the three-day training program, the participants will have accomplished the following:

- They will be trained on a work processing system that processes all incoming paperwork, email, voice messaging, verbal requests and thoughts and ideas from their own mind.
- *They will have all the above entered into their own work processing system.*
- They will have a design completed for furniture arrangement in their office space and five work regions established namely the paperwork region, computer region, telephone region, meeting region, and reference region.
- *They will have their furniture and equipment moved into their new assigned homes.*
- *They will have de-cluttered three or more boxes of paperwork/files.**
- *They will receive training on how to maintain their organized office space in two five-minute sessions a day.*
- They will receive a copy of this book to use for future reference.
- *They will have two desk drawers (not file drawers) de-cluttered.*
- *They will have custom drawer organizers installed in drawers.*
- *They will have new files created for four file drawers in their personal office space. The files will be installed into their drawers.*
- *They will learn skills in prioritizing, delegating, discarding, streamlining, follow-up, acting and scheduling.*
- Weekly Tele-coaching services are available to help them master the above mentioned habits and skills.

*The quantity of paper de-cluttered will depend on the speed at which the participant makes decisions. The quote of three boxes is what is anticipated for the participant that makes decisions at a moderate speed.

**Call now to schedule the dates for your own in-house training program.
Call (801)756-3382 or visit us at
www.OrganizeEnterprise.com today.**

---

*Ask Christi about her keynote, half day and one day training programs.

Christi also offers training for the home front.
Organize Your Home — so you can keep it clutter-free in <u>just 10 minutes</u> a day!

Have you ever organized spaces in your home only to have to organize it again a month or two later?

The Management Mentor™ teaches you seven strategies that cause your things to STAY organized.

You will be able to break free of chaos and clutter in the home. At the same time you'll be able to break free of hours and hours of maintenance. You'll learn organizing principles that cause your organization to last and specific application of those principles in organizing your paperwork, laundry, toys, games, videos, CDs and more.

You will cut your time spent dealing with those things by 50%!

This system has helped thousands of home owners be able to maintain a clutter-free and organized home in just 10 minutes a day.

<u>Course objectives:</u>

1. Introduce the seven strategies that cause your things to STAY organized.

2. Give examples of application for each strategy given.

3. Help the participants appreciate the necessity of doing all seven steps of the organizing process in order to create lasting change.

4. Describe the organizing principle of establishing a proper fit between your space & your things.

5. Describe the organizing principle of storing things at the place it is first used.

6. Introduce the organizing principle of making it easier to put an item away than it is to get out. Just barely!

7. Highlight the organizing principle of eliminating extra motions in the putting away process.

8. Describe the organizing principle of labeling.

9. Highlight the organizing principle of maintaining your systems daily.

10. Give demonstrations on how to apply the seven strategies with your paperwork, laundry, toys, games, videos, and CDs.

11. Introduce the seven steps of the organizing process.

12. Improve participant's motivation to get their homes organized by exploring the costs of clutter.

13. Clarify the participant's values as to life accomplishments and experiences. What do they really want? Help them set up activity regions that support them in what they value.

14. Establish the importance of working with their current habits instead of fighting against them.

15. Design a master plan of the home and the activity regions to set up in the home.

16. Describe how to speed sort. De-cluttering the home in a fraction of the time.

17. Give guidelines on how to assign the right home so as to reduce clutter and maintenance.

18. Give guidelines on how to choose the containers that minimize clutter and avoid the containers that cause your home to be cluttered.

19. Describe the 10 minute sweep that keeps your home clutter free.

20. Challenge the participants to choose their pace in which to work, start with something small, and transform their home one room at a time.

Need More In-Depth Help to Thoroughly De-Clutter Your Home?

Get Christi Youd's "30 Days to a Clutter-Free Home" Coaching Program!

Clutter can really take a toll on your sanity – let Christi show you how to do it correctly...step-by-step.

If clutter in your home is holding you and your family back from achieving the happiness and unity that you want to feel, then this program is designed to help YOU.

Christi will guide you every step of the way to clear out the clutter from every room in your home – GUARANTEED!

And as the clutter disappears, so will your feelings of anger, defeat, and being overwhelmed. This coaching program really works!

By tapping into Christi's expertise and experience through this coaching program, you'll actually be getting more of her for the money than if you hired her to do the work for you. It's the best win-win opportunity to clear out the clutter from your home once and for all!

For complete details about the "30 Days to a Clutter-Free Home" Coaching Program, see the back of this book for contact information.